# PAPERCRAFTS
## Around the World

Phyllis Fiarotta & Noel Fiarotta

Sterling Publishing Co., Inc.  New York

Edited by Jeanette Green

**Library of Congress Cataloging-in-Publication Data**

Fiarotta, Phyllis.
    Papercrafts around the world / by Phyllis Fiarotta and Noel
Fiarotta.
       p.    cm.
    Includes index.
    Summary: Provides background information and instructions for all
kinds of paper craft projects from different countries.
    ISBN 0-8069-3990-7
    1. Paper work—Juvenile literature.  [1. Paper work.
2. Handicraft.]  I. Fiarotta, Noel.  II. Title.
TT870.F53  1996                                       95-44154
745.54—dc20

3  5  7  9  10  8  6  4  2

First paperback edition published in 2000 by
Sterling Publishing Company, Inc.
387 Park Avenue South, New York, N.Y. 10016
© 1996 by Phyllis Fiarotta & Noel Fiarotta
Distributed in Canada by Sterling Publishing
*c/o* Canadian Manda Group, One Atlantic Avenue, Suite 105
Toronto, Ontario, Canada M6K 3E7
Distributed in Great Britain and Europe by Chris Lloyd
463 Ashley Road, Parkstone, Poole, Dorset, BH14 0AX, England
Distributed in Australia by Capricorn Link (Australia) Pty Ltd.
P.O. Box 6651, Baulkham Hills, Business Centre, NSW 2153, Australia
*Printed in China*

Sterling ISBN 0-8069-3990-7 Trade
0-8069-4986-4 Paper

*Dedicated to the memory of our mother, Santa Fiarotta,*
*more than flesh and bone, an exquisite work of art*

# CONTENTS

# PAPER

Imagine life without paper. You would have no books to read, no birthday cards to receive, and no loose-leaf paper for homework assignments. Paper, in all its colors, textures, and uses, is important in every part of your daily life.

The history of paper is multicultural. The early Egyptians made a type of writing paper from the papyrus plant, from which comes the word *paper*. Papyrus went from Egypt to ancient Rome and Greece. Eventually, a different kind of paper called *parchment,* made from calfskin, took the place of papyrus. Rag paper was used for early printed books. Paper made from wood fiber, that we use today, was first produced in China.

The earliest uses of paper were for letters, business transactions, and recording important events. As people became more adventurous, they used paper in creative ways, fashioning kites to catch the wind, beads to thread on string, and masks to wear during Mardi Gras.

With the first snip of your scissors, you can begin a creative journey into the cultures and celebrations of your sisters and brothers around the world. Bon voyage!

# PICTURES

# SILHOUETTES
## *France*

Portraits and scenes cut from paper date back to ancient Greece. Today's silhouette gets its name from the Frenchman Étienne de Silhouette, who, in the early 1700s, was famous for his free-cut portraits as well as his frugality. In England, when Queen Victoria reigned, silhouettes were called shades or shadow portraits.

1. Collect your supplies: black and colored paper, crayons, scissors, and paste.
2. Draw the profile of a person or animal on black paper with a crayon. Practice first on scrap paper.
3. Cut out the profile.
4. Paste the silhouette on white or on a light-colored paper.
5. If you wish, frame the silhouette with a paper frame. The one shown here has an oval opening and colored paper designs.

# NIGHTSCAPES
## *United States*

In the late 1800s, people brightened their dark homes with window pictures. A window picture is a silhouette with colored tissue paper behind cut-out areas. Popular window pictures were landscapes at night.

1. Collect your supplies: black paper, crayons, scissors, colored tissue paper, paste, nail, and tape.
2. With a crayon, draw hills, trees, bushes, and a house with windows on black paper (A). Draw a frame around the scene (arrow in A).
3. Cut out the sky and windows from the landscape (gray areas in A).
4. Flip the night scene over.
5. Paste yellow tissue paper over the windows. Paste blue tissue over the sky area (B). If you don't have yellow and blue tissue, use white gift-wrap tissue and color it with markers.
6. Create stars by carefully making holes in the sky with a nail.
7. Tape or hang the finished picture in a window.

# TANGRAM
## *China*

A *tangram* is a puzzle pieced together with seven specific geometric shapes, called tans, cut from a square. These seven tans can be recombined to create thousands of new designs. Edgar Allan Poe and Lewis Carroll tested their imaginations with Chinese tangrams.

1. Collect your supplies: paper, pencil, ruler, and scissors.
2. Draw a large, perfect square on colored paper. Red is the traditional color.
3. With a pencil and ruler, draw lines on the square exactly like those on the red square shown. If you wish, trace the square and lines directly from the book for patterns.
4. Cut out the geometric shapes.
5. Create your own tangrams or follow the examples shown. Geometric shapes should touch each other but not overlap. Shown are A—cat, B—dog, C—seal, D—fish, E—rooster, F—horse, G—bird, H—goose, I—rabbit, J—fox, K—camel.

# PINPRICKING
## *China*

Pinpricking is the art of making tiny holes in paper, which allow light to pass through. The earliest pinpricking comes from the Chinese celebration of Yuan Hsiao, the festival of lanterns. Red paper lamps had pinpricked lucky characters that said "happiness" and "prosperity." In the Colonial United States, shades decorated with pinpricking were used for oil lamps. Hang a pinpricked picture in a window or make a cover for a lampshade.

1. Collect your supplies: small white, flat lampshade; colored or brown wrapping paper; tape; scissors; pencil; markers; large needle or thin nail; and glue.
2. Wrap paper around a small lampshade and tape it in place (A).
3. Trim away the extra paper at the top and bottom of the shade (B). Trim some paper where it overlaps (arrow in B).
4. Remove the paper taped to the lampshade. Draw a design in a light pencil line.
5. Color the drawing with markers (C).
6. Punch holes into the paper with a needle or nail, following the pencil lines (C).
7. Glue the cover onto the lampshade.

# HUANG-HUA WINDOW FLOWERS
## *China*

In China, paper cuts decorate lanterns, fans, and containers. Because people often displayed them on window glass, they called them window flowers, even if they were not flower designs. *Huang-hua* means "yellow flower." Window flowers are cut from colored paper or white rice paper, then painted with bright colors.

1. Collect your supplies: colored paper, pencil, scissors, watercolor paints, paintbrush, and glass of water.

2. Draw a flower, animal, butterfly, or fish design on paper. If you wish, trace the fish design shown or trace a design from a coloring book.

3. Cut out the design. For the fish design, cut along the dotted lines to cut out the inside areas.

4. Place the cutout on a piece of paper and brush it with a lot of water.

5. While the paper is wet, quickly brush on different colors. The colors will bleed into each other.

# MARBLING
## *Iran*

Shortly after the Persians (in what is now Iran) created marbled paper in 1550, the craft found its way to Europe. Eventually, early bookbinders added marbled papers to the inside covers of books. Because books were made entirely of handmade sheets of paper, only rich people could buy them. When machines began to mass produce books, printed marbled paper took the place of handmade paper.

1. Collect your supplies: paper, artist's oil paint, turpentine, and a large disposable aluminum baking pan or a large plastic bowl.
2. Fill a pan or bowl three-fourths full with water.
3. In a paper cup, mix together small amounts of paint and turpentine. The more turpentine you add, the less bright the color will be. Ask an adult to help whenever you use turpentine. Mix 2 or more cups of different colors.
4. Add a spoonful of each color to the water (A).
5. With a spoon, stir the floating paints once or twice to create a swirled design (B).
6. Lay an end of a piece of paper on the water, at one end of the pan or bowl. Roll the entire paper onto the water (C).
7. Quickly lift the paper and lay it on a table to dry, paint side up.

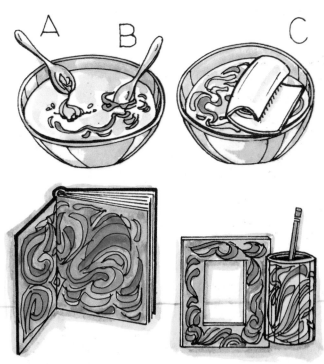

8. Paste marbled papers on a book's inside covers or around a coffee can for a pencil holder. Make colorful frames for a photograph or drawing.

# SCROLL FRAME
## *Switzerland*

In Switzerland, before printed greeting cards, people created handmade cards framed with curlicue borders called scrolls. Holidays, especially New Year's Day, were popular times to send scrolled cards.

1. Collect your supplies: paper, pencil, scissors, and paste.
2. Fold a sheet of paper in half (A). Fold the paper in half again (B).
3. Draw a curlicue design along the two unfolded sides (C).
4. Cut out the scroll design (C). Open the paper.
5. Paste the scroll on a sheet of paper. If you wish, paste on colored paper designs.
6. Write a greeting or draw a picture inside the scroll border.

A

B

C

# GEOMETRIC CUTS

# GWIAZDY
## *Poland*

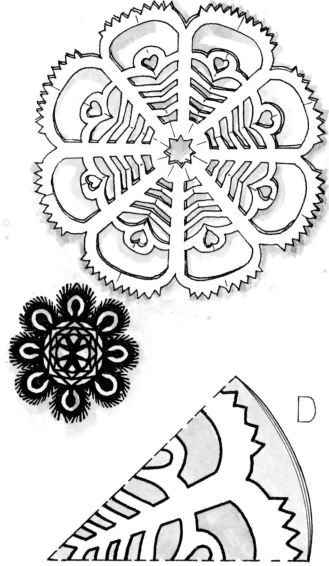

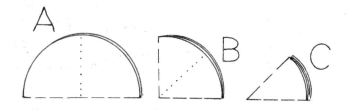

*Gwiazdy* means "stars." This paper cut is from the Kurpie and Lowicz regions of Poland. Most gwiazdy designs are geometric, but some include birds or butterflies. Like snowflakes, no two gwiazdy appear exactly alike.

1. Collect your supplies: paper, compass, pencil, and scissors.

2. Draw a large circle on colored paper with a compass, or trace around a small dish. Cut out.

3. Fold the circle in half (A) and in half two more times (B and C).

4. Draw different shapes on the folded sides (broken lines D).

5. Cut out the drawn shapes (shaded areas in D). Open the circle.

# MONI-KIRI CRESTS
## *Japan*

*Moni kiri,* which means "crest cutting," dates back a thousand years. Crests decorated cloth and other household things. Flowers and geometric shapes are popular designs. Make the designs shown or design your own moni-kiri crest for your family. Traditional moni kiri fits inside a square, but your crest can fit inside any shape.

1. Collect your supplies: black and white paper, pencil or crayons, scissors, and paste.
2. Cut a square, rectangle, or circle from white or black paper.
3. Fold the paper in half, then in half one or two more times (A and B).
4. Draw a design that includes both folded sides (broken lines in C and D.)

5. Cut out the design. Open the paper.
6. Paste the crest on its opposite color of paper.

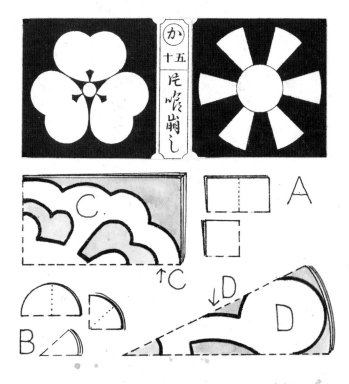

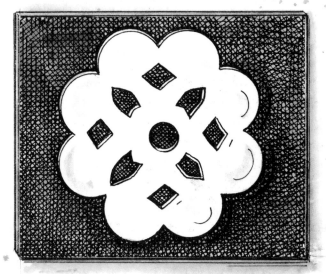

# FIESTA FLAGS
## *Mexico*

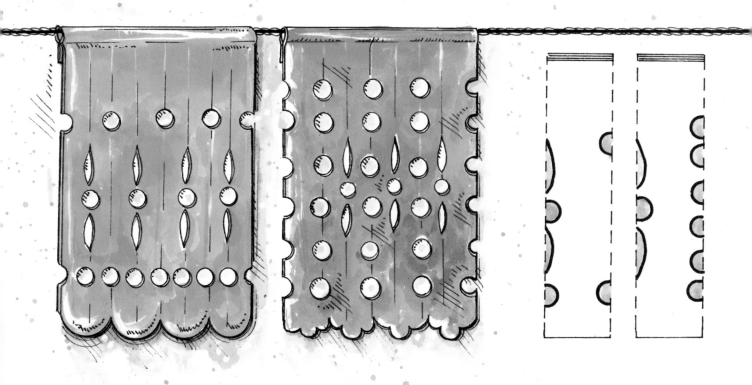

In Mexico, everyone loves a *fiesta,* the Spanish word for "festival." People decorate the streets with lacy tissue paper flags. Cutout designs can be simple circles or fancy pictures. Some flags are large enough to cover tables and church altars. For a family or school celebration, crisscross fiesta flags above the guests' heads.

1. Collect your supplies: colored tissue paper, scissors, paste, and string.

2. Cut colored or white tissue paper into flag-size rectangles. You can also use construction paper or cellophane wrap.
3. Fold a rectangle in half several times.
4. Cut out circles or geometric shapes along the folded sides (shaded areas on diagrams). Open the paper.
5. Fold an edge of the flag over a length of string and paste it in place.
6. Attach many flags to the string to create a festive display.

# KLAUSJAGEN MITER
## *Switzerland*

On December 6, in the Swiss town Kussnacht am Rigi, people enjoy the parade of Klausjagen, or St. Nicholas. Horns blow and bells ring as marchers wear giant hats called miters, with cut-out designs lit from inside by candles. Above is an example of a cut-out design. Make Klausjagen hats for your next birthday or New Year's Eve party.

1. Collect your supplies: colored paper, crayons, scissors, and paste.
2. Fold a sheet of paper in half (A).
3. Draw a curved line from a corner on the folded side to the opposite side (A).
4. Cut away the corner (shaded area in A).
5. Fold the paper in half two more times (B and C).
6. Draw different shapes only along the side with the double fold (arrow in C).
7. Cut out the shapes. Open the paper.
8. Roll a strip of paper into a ring to fit around your head. Paste closed.
9. Paste the cut-out paper to the ring.

# WINDOW PICTURES
## *England*

In the late 1800s in England, most people covered their windows with heavy curtains. Paper window pictures brightened windows that were not covered. Create a kaleidoscope of colors for the windows in your home.

1. Collect your supplies: colored tissue paper, scissors, paste, and tape.
2. From tissue paper, cut three squares the same size, each a different color. If you do not have colored tissue, color white gift-wrap tissue with markers.

3. Fold each square in half from corner to corner (A). Fold each in half two more times (B and C).
4. Draw shapes along the folded sides of each square (dotted lines in D).
5. Cut out all shapes (gray areas in D).
6. Open the squares (E).
7. Paste the three papers together at their corners. Tape the window picture to a window.

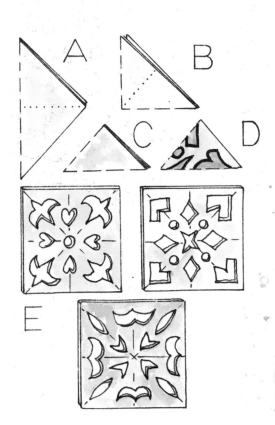

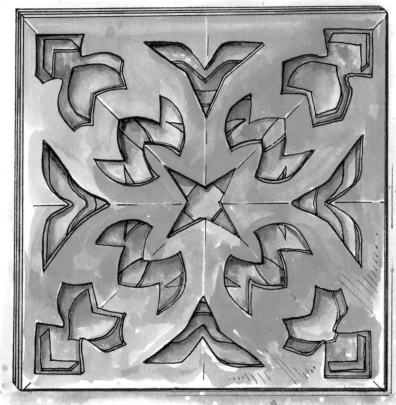

# GLOW LAMP
## *China*

Before electricity came into homes in China, lanterns lit the night. The hanging paper lanterns were as intricate as a dragonfly with flapping wings, while table lamps were simple tubes. Make a glow lamp to light a backyard barbecue, a family camp-out, or the T.V. room.

1. Collect your supplies: colored paper, white tissue paper, scissors, paste, markers, glass jar, and a small candle.
2. Fold black or dark-colored paper in half many times along the width.
3. Cut out triangles along the folded sides (shaded areas in A). Open the paper.
4. Paste tissue paper on the cut-out paper, covering all the cut-out areas (B).
5. Color the tissue over the cutouts with markers (C).
6. Place a small candle inside a tall jar or glass (D).
7. Roll the paper around the jar with the tissue paper inside (E). Paste (F).
8. Ask an adult to light the candle.

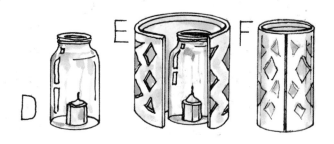

# CONFETTI
## *Italy*

*Confetti* is the Italian word for "candies" or "confections." In the late Middle Ages these candies were small, hard sugar plums people tossed during carnivals. Today in Italy, confetti shops offer colorful candies, party favors, and decorations for all occasions, from religious feasts to weddings.

The confetti we know is tiny bits of paper we throw to create a shower of color at parties. Create your own confetti for the next time you cry "Surprise!"

1. Collect your supplies: colored construction paper, tissue paper, specialty papers, or colored photographs from magazines; scissors; and a paper punch.
2. For same-size squares (A), cut paper into many narrow strips. Gather the strips and cut across them.
3. For punched circles (B), punch circles from paper with a paper punch.
4. For different size squares (C), cut paper into different widths of strips. Gather the strips and cut across them.
5. For irregular shapes (D), collect scrap paper from all your papercraft projects. Chop it into little pieces.

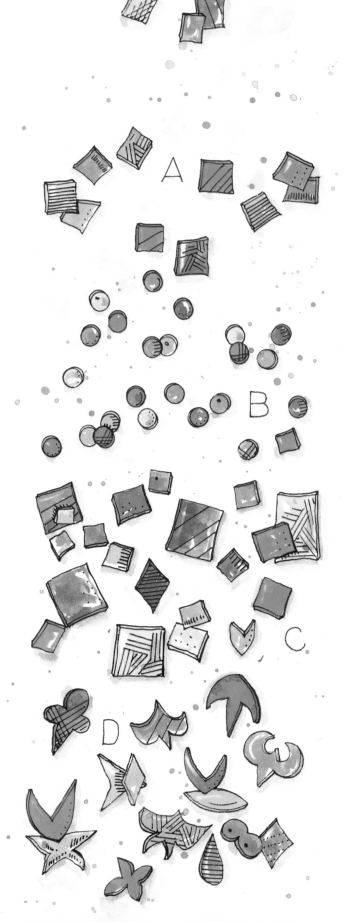

# MIRROR IMAGES

# LEAF CUTS
## *Canada*

The early settlers of eastern Canada made paper leaf cuts to decorate their homes and to remind themselves of spring during long, cold winters. You'll find tree and bush leaves unique to where you live. Gather a collection of leaves and duplicate their shapes in paper cuts.

1. Collect your supplies: colored paper, scissors, pencil, and paste.
2. Cut a large green paper square and a smaller brown paper square.
3. Fold both squares in half from corner to corner (A). Fold in half two more times (B and C).
4. On the longest folded side, draw half an acorn on the brown paper (D) and half an oak leaf on the green paper (E). The bottom of each must include some of the other folded side (arrow in D and E).
5. Cut out the leaf and the acorn. Open the papers.
6. Paste the acorns to the center of the leaves.
7. Hang the leaf cut as is or paste it on paper.

24

# FLORAL MOSAIC
## *Uzbekistan*

Uzbekistan is a Central Asian country that was once a stop on the route where caravans of camels carried silk from the Orient to Europe. Most of Uzbekistan's ancient buildings are covered with blue, green, and yellow tiles in beautiful patterns. Whether mosaic tile designs are geometric or like the traditional flower patterns shown, craftspeople first create them in paper.

1. Collect your supplies: colored paper, compass, pencil, scissors, and paste.

2. Draw a large circle on blue paper with a compass. Draw a larger circle on yellow paper. You can also trace around dishes.
3. Cut out the circles.
4. Fold the blue circle in half three times.
5. Draw designs on the folded sides similar to the ones shown (D).
6. Cut out the designs. Open each.
7. Paste the center design on the center of the yellow circle. Paste the flowers and leaves around the center design.

# FLOWER MOTIFS
## *Switzerland*

During the 1800s in Switzerland, artists decorated birth certificates, declarations of love, and New Year's wishes with colorful paper cuts. Nature inspired most of the designs. The tulip and the carnation were the most popular.

1. Collect your supplies: white and colored paper, pencil, scissors, watercolor paints, paintbrush, glass of water, and paste.
2. Fold a sheet of white paper in half along the length.
3. On the folded side, draw half of a carnation with leaves (A), a tulip with leaves (B), or any flower you wish.
4. Cut out the flower. Open the paper.
5. Place the flower on a sheet of paper.
6. Brush water on the entire flower and quickly paint on colors. Dry.
7. Paste the flower on paper. Frame with a paper frame.

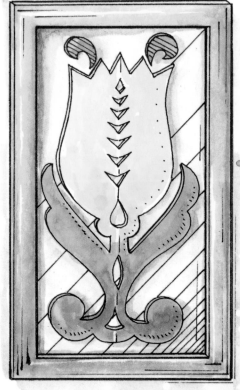

# SCHERENSCHNITTE
## *Germany*

*Scherenschnitte* means "scissor cut" or "silhouette" in German. This paper craft dates back to the mid-1600s. A popular design was a nature scene inside a heart. The Swiss, in the 1800s, also created black silhouette scenes in hearts. Their paper cuts were more intricate than the German form, as in the design at the top of the page.

1. Collect your supplies: colored paper, pencil, and scissors.
2. Fold a sheet of colored paper in half.
3. Draw half a heart on the folded side. Create the heart with the daisy as shown, or make your own design.
4. Cut out the heart. Open the paper.
5. Leave the heart as is or paste it on paper.

# SEED SPIRITS
## *Mexico*

In San Pablito, Mexico, an important ceremony is the baptism of the seeds. In spring when the crops are planted, villagers make paper seed spirits. Spirits represent such things as corn, coffee, and honeybees. Village officials keep the paper cuts through the growing season to safeguard the harvest.

1. Collect your supplies: light-colored paper, pencil, scissors, watercolor paints, paintbrush, and glass of water.
2. Fold a sheet of paper in half along the width.
3. Draw half a figure on the folded side, as shown in the diagram. Leave room above the head.
4. Draw leaves and fruits on the top of the head and at the sides of the hands and legs (areas shown in light gray in the diagram). Choose a pomegranate (shown on the seed spirit), a pear (A), a pineapple (B), or your own favorite fruit.
5. Cut out the seed spirit. Open the paper.
6. Paint the leaves and the fruit.
7. Leave the seed spirit as is or paste it on paper.

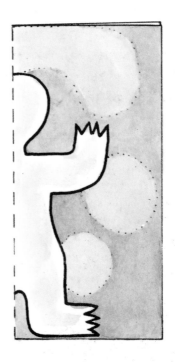

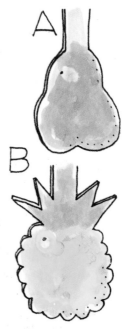

# PINEAPPLE QUILT
## *United States*

In the 1800s, American missionaries introduced both fabric and the appliqué quilt to Hawaii. Nature inspires Hawaiian quilt designs, like the ginger plant and the pineapple. Stitches, sewn on a quilt around the appliqué designs, represent the water surrounding the islands. Quilters first make designs on paper for their patterns.

1. Collect your supplies: colored paper, pencil, scissors, and paste.
2. Cut two green and two yellow paper squares all the same size. To make the ginger plant shown above, use pink instead of yellow paper.
3. Fold the squares in half from corner to corner.
4. On the folded sides, draw leaves on the green papers and half of a pineapple on the yellow papers.
5. Cut out the designs. Open the papers.
6. On a large light blue sheet of paper that represents the ocean, paste on the pineapples and leaves as shown.

# RIBANDS
## *Poland*

The *riband* is one of Poland's oldest paper crafts. Ribands decorate Polish homes and sometimes take the place of ribbons on a bridal bouquet. The two-streamer riband is from the Sannicki region, and the three-streamer is from the Pultusk region.

1. Collect your supplies: colored paper, compass, scissors, and paste.
2. With a compass, draw three different sizes of circles, each on a different color of paper.
3. Fold the circles in half and cut out designs along the edges (A).
4. To make the medallion, paste the circles on top of each (B).
5. Cut two or three paper streamers and decorate as shown (C), or create your own.
6. Paste the streamers to the back of the medallion.

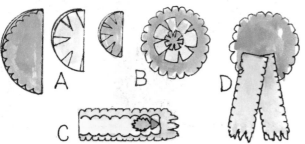

# WYCINANKI
## *Poland*

*Wycinanki* is a traditional Polish folk art. In past times, country folk cut intricate mirror-image designs from paper. Roosters, flowers, and geometric shapes were popular designs. At Easter and Christmas, people painted the inside of their homes with white paint and hung the paper cuts on the walls and along the beams of the ceiling. Today's wycinanki uses popular designs, like the Christmas tree seen on greeting cards.

1. Collect your supplies: colored paper, pencil, scissors, and paste.
2. Fold green paper in half. Fold a small piece of red paper in half.
3. Draw half a tree on the folded side of the green paper (A). Draw a tree stand on the folded side of the red paper (B).
4. Cut out the tree and the stand. Open the papers.
5. Paste the tree and the stand to a sheet of paper with a tree trunk between them.
6. Cut out tree ornaments and flowers, each two exactly alike. For ornaments on the center of the tree, like the star, only one is needed.
7. Paste the ornaments on the tree. Ornaments on the left side should balance those on the right.

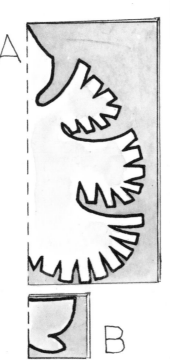

# COAT OF ARMS
## *Switzerland*

In Switzerland in the 1700s, craftspeople cut intricate patterns for door knockers and keyhole plates. They also cut paper into coats of arms to be used for marriage licenses, birth certificates, and business transactions. Create your own family coat-of-arms design and use it as writing paper or a family shield to hang on the wall.

1. Collect your supplies: colored paper, pencil, scissors, and paste.
2. Fold a large sheet of colored paper in half along the length.
3. Draw half a coat of arms on the folded side of the paper. Copy the design shown or create your own.
4. Cut out the coat of arms. Open the paper.
5. Paste on your family name and designs cut from colored paper.
6. To make writing paper, cut your coat of arms from typing paper.

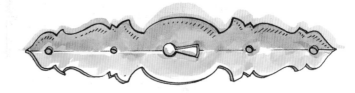

# ACCORDION FOLDS

# OCHTER-FOGGEL
## *United States*

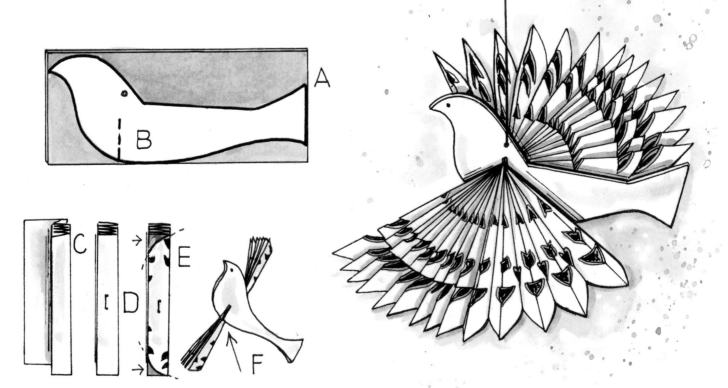

The Pennsylvania Dutch are not originally from Holland but from Germany. The word *deutsch,* which means "German," was mistaken for the word *Dutch.* The Pennsylvania "Dutch" are known for their folk art. The paper bird, *ochter-foggel,* is a sign of good luck when hung in a window or tree.

1. Collect your supplies: construction paper, tissue paper, pencil, scissors, stapler, and string.
2. Draw the bird's body on construction paper (study A). Cut out.
3. Cut a slit into the bottom of the bird (B). Make a small hole above the slit.
4. Cut a tissue paper square twice as large as the body.
5. Fold the square back and forth. The folds should be small and the same size (C).
6. To make the wings, staple the folded paper in the middle (D). Cut away a corner at each end and cut out shapes on the sides (E).
7. Open the paper to form the wings.
8. Insert the wings into the slit (F).
9. Tie string into the hole and hang.

# SUNBURST
## *Sweden*

The sunburst is a popular design for Christmas ornaments in Sweden. Because the number of folds and cuts vary, no two sunbursts are alike. Make sunbursts in white and metallic papers for the Christmas tree, or in yellow and orange to hang in a window on a sunny day.

1. Collect your supplies: paper, scissors, paste or glue, and string.
2. Cut a piece of paper much longer than it is wide.
3. Fold the paper back and forth. The folds should be small and the same size.
4. Staple the folded paper in the middle (A).
5. Cut away the corners and cut out shapes along the sides, as described in the Ochter-Foggel.
6. Open the paper on both sides of the staple to form fans (B).
7. Glue or paste the fans together to form a circle (C).
8. Tie string into a cut-out shape and hang.

# BUTTERFLY
## *Mexico*

Mexico is known for paper decorations used in many fiestas. This pretty butterfly has wings made from two pleated squares. Add a third square and the butterfly turns into a star or a snowflake.

1. Collect your supplies: colored paper, scissors, paste or glue, glitter, and string.
2. Cut two paper squares in different colors for the wings. Also cut a narrow strip of paper for the body.
3. Fold the squares back and forth from corner to corner (A). The folds should be small and the same size.
4. Place the folded papers together and wrap the strip around the middle (B). Paste in place.
5. Open the folded paper on both sides of the body to form fans (C).
6. Glue or paste the fans together to form the butterfly's wings (D).
7. Glue glitter on the wings.
8. Tie string to the butterfly and hang.
9. To make a star, use three folded paper squares.

# WEIHNACHT ANGEL
## *Germany*

The angel is one of the earliest ornaments for the German Christmas tree. When trees were lit by candles instead of electric lights, angels with foil-paper skirts reflected the light of the flickering flames.

1. Collect your supplies: colored or foil paper, scissors, stapler, white glue, markers, and string.
2. Fold a sheet of colored or foil paper back and forth (A). The folds should be small and the same size.
3. Staple the folded paper at one end to form the skirt (B).
4. Cut a paper square for the collar. Cut slits into two sides (C).
5. Draw wings on paper (D). Cut out.
6. Squeeze a lot of white glue on one side of the collar and the wings (E).
7. Lay the stapled end of the skirt on the glued wings (F). Lay the glued side of the collar on top of the skirt (G). Dry.
8. Draw a head on paper. Cut it out.
9. Glue the head to the collar.
10. Tie string into a small hole made at the top of the head. Hang.

# PORTRAIT CASE
## *England*

A Frenchman named Joseph Niepce made the first photograph in the early 1800s. As photographs improved through the years, people visited photographers' studios to have their portraits taken. In England, paper folders displayed a collection of family portraits printed on paper or tin.

1. Collect your supplies: colored paper, ruler, pencil, scissors, and paste.
2. Cut two very long pieces of paper in two different colors.
3. Divide both papers into four equal sections by folding each in half and in half again (A).
4. Cut one paper along the folds (B).
5. Draw a window inside a section (C). Cut out to make a frame (D).
6. Add paste to all but the top edge of the frame (E). Do not spread the paste up to the window.
7. Place the frame on the uncut paper over the first folded section (F). The unglued side is at the top.
8. Paste on the remaining frames.
9. Cut special drawings, pictures from magazines, and photographs a little larger than the windows. Slip them into the frames.

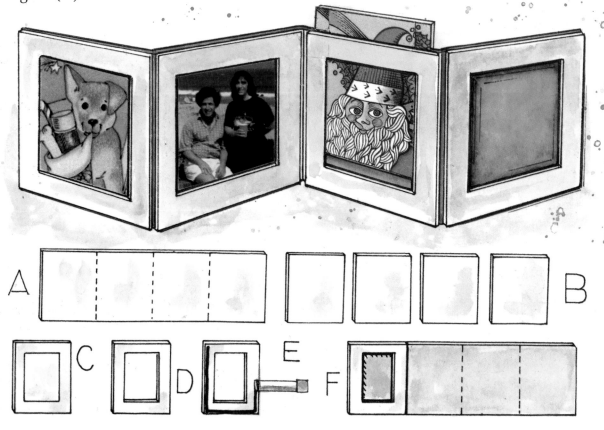

# DANCING DOLLIES
## United States

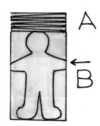

Dancing dollies, known as paper doll chains, are an old folk craft enjoyed by children. It was once popular with sailors, who spent a long time on ships. Be creative and make paper chains of daisies, elephants, or birthday cakes.

1. Collect your supplies: colored paper, pencil, scissors, and markers.
2. Cut a very long strip of paper. If you wish, paste strips together.
3. Fold the paper back and forth (A). The folds should be the same size and wide enough for a drawing.
4. Draw a girl or a boy with arms touching the folded sides (B).
5. Cut out the girl or boy. The folded paper at the end of the arms must not be cut away. Open the paper.
6. To make birthday party invitations, draw a cake with candles following the instructions for the doll. Color the candles and write your message with markers.

# WASHBOARD CAT
## *United States*

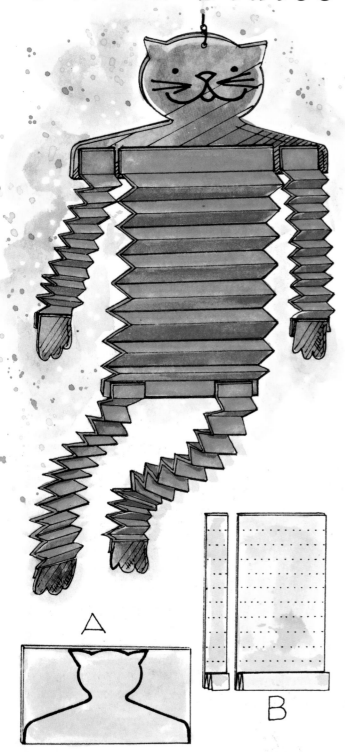

A

B

English-American children, dressing in each other's clothing on All Hallows Eve, wore the first Halloween costumes. The Native American custom of lighting hollowed-out pumpkins to ward off bad spirits were the first jack-o'-lanterns. Irish-American farmers began the custom of trick or treat. The washboard cat is a more recent addition to the holiday of Halloween celebrated in the United States and Canada.

1. Collect your supplies: colored paper, pencil, scissors, markers, and paste or glue.
2. Draw a cat's head and shoulders on a black or dark-colored paper (A). Also draw hands and feet. Cut out.
3. Create a cat's face with markers or colored paper.
4. From orange paper, cut four narrow strips for the arms and legs and a wide strip for the body (B). The body and arms should fit on the cat's shoulders.
5. Fold all the papers back and forth. The folds should be small and the same size.
6. Paste hands and feet to the arms and legs.
7. Paste the body and arms to the cat's shoulders and the legs to the body.

# CREATIVE FOLDS

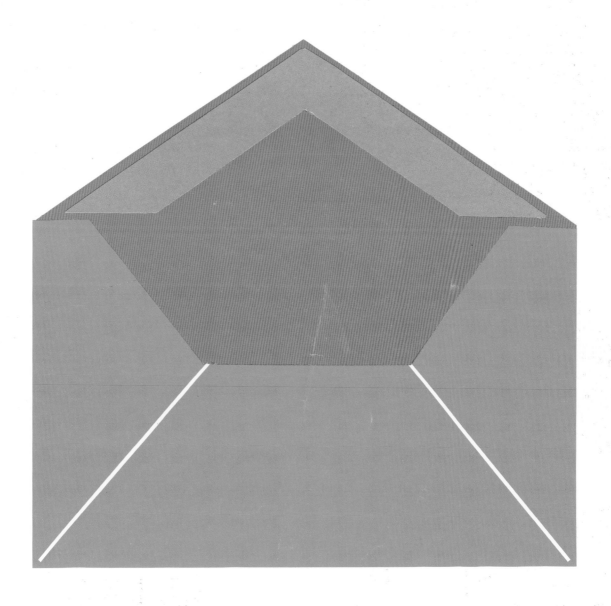

# TANABATA MATSURI TASSEL
## *Japan*

Tanabata Matsuri, the star festival, is celebrated in Japan in July or August. In front of their homes, people display bamboo branches decorated with paper dolls, tassels, and origami. The decorations symbolize success in weaving, writing, and handicrafts. At the end of the holiday, people toss the branches into rivers, to float to the sea.

1. Collect your supplies: colored paper, scissors, string, and tube macaroni.
2. Cut colored paper into squares.
3. Fold a square in half from corner to corner. Open and fold in the opposite direction (broken lines in A).
4. Turn the square over.
5. Fold the square in half from side to side. Open and fold it in half in the opposite direction (broken lines in B).
6. Turn the square over.
7. Push the sides toward the center (arrows in C) to form a bell, which has two triangles (D).
8. Cut off the tip of the bell (arrow in D).
9. Tie a tube macaroni to the end of a length of string (E).
10. Thread the bell onto string. Rest the bell on the macaroni.
11. Keep tying on macaroni and adding bells along the length of string.

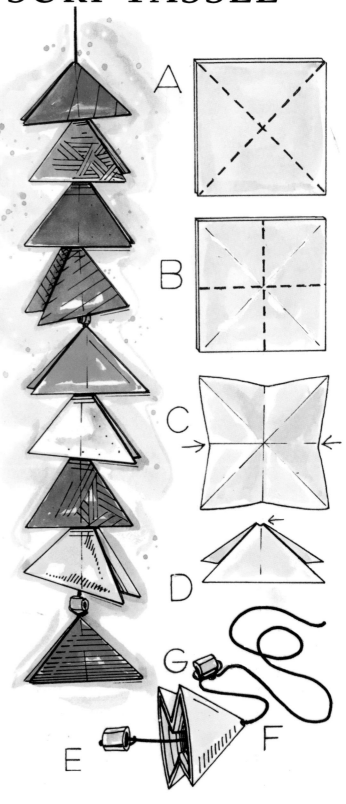

# ORIGAMI BOX
## *Japan*

Origami first appeared in Japan in the 1100s. Origami is the folding of paper into birds, animals, and objects that are used in festivals, ceremonies, and entertainment. Traditional origami uses 4-inch or 6-inch paper squares, although squares can be so tiny that some folded designs can actually fit on the head of a pin.

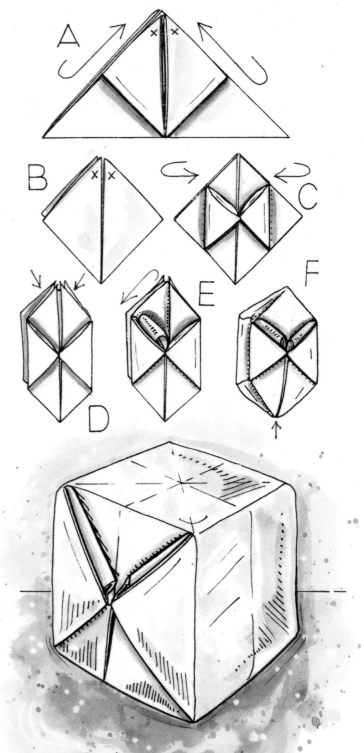

1. Collect your supplies: thin and lightweight paper (typing paper) and scissors.
2. Cut out a very large paper square.
3. Fold the square into a bell as described in the Tanabata Tassel project. The bell has two triangles, an upper and a lower.
4. Place the bell on the table with the longest side at the bottom.
5. Bring the bottom points of the upper triangle to the top point (see the *X*'s in A).
6. Turn the paper over.
7. Repeat with the remaining two bottom points (B).
8. Fold over the two side points to form pockets (study C).
9. Turn the paper over.
10. Repeat with the remaining side points (D). Four separate wings are at the top (arrows in D).
11. Fold down all four wings and push their tips into the pocket below them (E).
12. Blow into the opening at the bottom (arrow in F). Help mold the box with your fingers as it fills with air.

# YUAN TAN ENVELOPE
## *China*

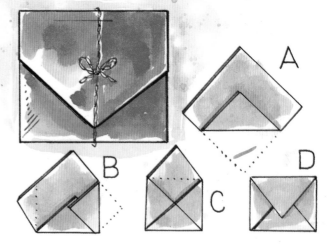

Yuan Tan, the Chinese New Year or Lunar Festival, is celebrated in late January or in February. A long paper dragon, operated by many handlers, dances down the streets, visiting each store. The merchants give the dragon red envelopes containing money donations.

1. Collect your supplies: red paper, scissors, and yarn or string.
2. Cut red paper into a large square.
3. Bring the bottom corner more than half way up and press flat (A). Bring the side corners to the middle (B and C) and the top corner down (D).
4. Tie the envelope closed with yarn or string.

# PUZZLE PURSE
## *United States*

Long before there were valentine cards, young men in the Pennsylvania Dutch community gave puzzle purses to their sweethearts, as tokens of love. A puzzle purse, a sheet of paper folded many times, reveals a different picture or message when each new fold is opened.

1. Collect your supplies: paper, scissors, and crayons or markers.
2. Cut a piece of paper into a square.
3. Draw a design on the square (A).
4. Bring the four corners to the middle and press flat, forming triangles.
5. Draw designs on the triangles (B).
6. Bring the new four corners to the middle and press flat.
7. Draw designs on the triangles (C).
8. Open the purse to see the designs.

# LOY KRATHONG BOAT
## *Thailand*

In mid-November, the Thai people gather at the waters' edge to celebrate the festival of Loy Krathong, which means "floating lotus cups." Canals, rivers, ponds, and pools turn the night into twinkling gardens of light. Families and friends gather to float lotus-shaped paper boats that contain lit candles. The people believe the boats carry away their problems.

1. Collect your supplies: paper and scissors.
2. Cut a large sheet of paper into a square. Use a grocery bag if you wish.
3. Fold the square in half from corner to corner. Open the square and fold it in half in the opposite direction (broken lines in A). The middle is where the fold marks cross.
4. Bring the four corners to the middle point to form triangles. Press flat (B).
5. Bring the new four corners to the middle point to form triangles. Press flat (C).
6. Lift the top triangles straight up.
7. Lift the lower triangles just a little. Notice that there is a crease on each triangle. Make these triangles pointier by making the creases sharper.

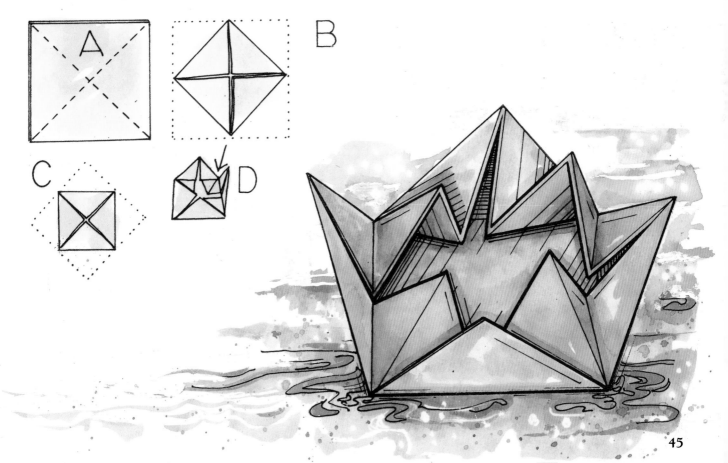

# POPPER
## *United States*

Before there were toy stores as big as football fields, children made their own toys from shoe boxes, ice cream sticks, and newspapers. Some favorite newspaper playthings were hats, boats, fringe trees, and the Fourth of July popper.

1. Collect your supplies: newspaper.
2. With the folded edge of a full sheet of newspaper at the top, fold the paper in half along the length (A). Open.
3. Fold the four corners to the crease line (B).
4. Fold the paper in half along the length (C).
5. Fold the paper in half along the width, forming two wings (D).
6. Fold the top wing down (study E). Repeat with the other wing.
7. To pop the popper, hold the points between your thumb and index finger and snap your wrist sharply.

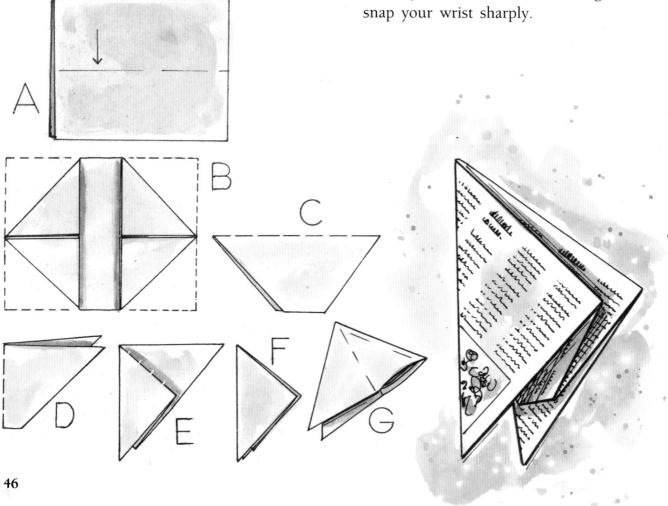

# NINGYO DOLL
## *Japan*

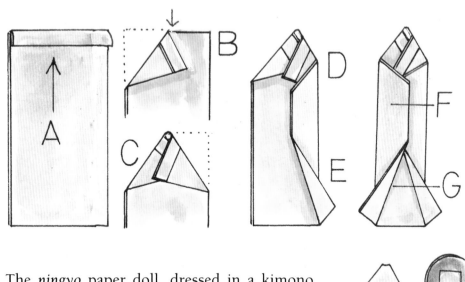

The *ningyo* paper doll, dressed in a kimono, has a magical purpose. According to tradition, if a person touches this doll, all the bad spirits in his or her body go into it. Once the ningyo doll takes the bad spirits, the person throws it into the river so that it is carried to the sea.

1. Collect your supplies: colored paper, scissors, crayons or markers, paste, and a toothpick.
2. Cut out two different colors of paper rectangles the same size.
3. With the two papers on top of each other, fold a little of the top edge over (arrow in A).
4. Turn the papers over. The folded edge is on the underside.
5. At the middle point on the folded edge (arrow in B), fold over the left corner.
6. Fold the right corner over the left corner (C).

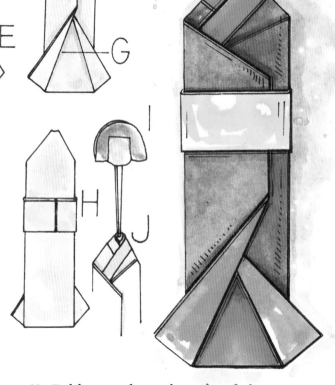

7. Fold over the right side of the papers (D). Fold out the right bottom corner (study E). Repeat with the left side (F and G).
8. Wrap a paper strip around the middle. Paste in place at the back (H).
9. Draw a simple head on paper. Cut it out and glue it to an end of a toothpick (I).
10. Push the toothpick into the top opening of the kimono (J).

# LENTEN CALENDAR
## *Greece*

Before there were printed calendars, the people of Greece hung a Lenten counter on a wall, to keep track of the seven weeks before Easter. This homemade calendar was a paper cutout of a nun with folded arms and seven feet. She had no mouth, which reminded people of their fasting. Every Saturday, the nun lost a foot, marking the passing of a week.

1. Collect your supplies: colored paper, pencil, scissors, and crayons or markers.
2. On colored paper, draw the nun as shown. Draw the outstretched arms shown in broken lines. You can trace the figure from the book. Cut it out.
3. Add crayon, marker, or paper designs on the skirt. Draw a face with no mouth.
4. Fold the arms over so that the hands overlap.

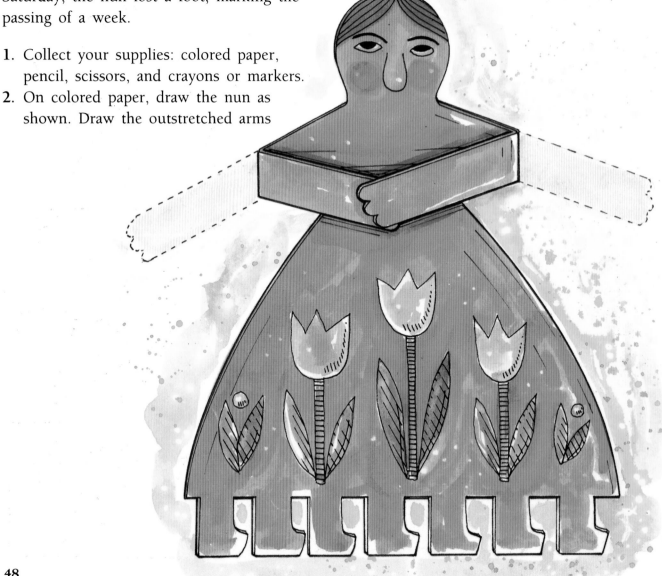

# KALANDA STAR
## *Greece*

On New Year's Day, the people of Greece honor St. Basil, one of the greatest fathers of the Orthodox Church. Children, along with their parents, go from house to house carrying an apple and a paper star or a paper ship. They sing the "Kalanda," which is a song of good wishes. The lady of the house gives the children coins, which they push into their apples.

1. Collect your supplies: paper, compass, scissors, ruler, and string.
2. Draw a large circle on paper with a compass. You can also trace around a plate. Cut it out.
3. Fold the circle in half and mark the middle point on the folded edge (arrow in A).
4. With a pencil and ruler, divide the half circle into five equal sections from the middle point (broken lines in A). A protractor will help you make equal sections.
5. Fold over two sections. One section remains uncovered (see the *x* in B).
6. Fold over the remaining section (see the *x* in C).
7. Fold the paper in half (D).
8. Cut away the top curve (E). The steeper the angle of the cut, the pointier the star.

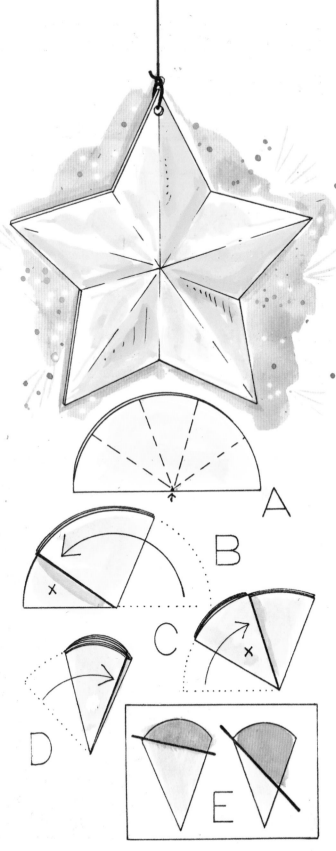

49

# HOSHOSHI FOLD & DYE
## *Japan*

The Japanese create beautiful dyed papers using absorbent papers with names like *gasenchi*, *torinokogami*, and *minogami*. People use dyed papers to wrap spices and books and to decorate religious shrines.

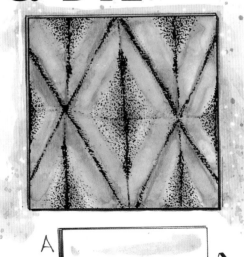

1. Collect your supplies: absorbent papers or paper towels, water, food coloring, and cups.
2. Fold a sheet of paper in half along the length and then in half again (A).
3. Fold the paper in half along the width (B) and in half again (C).
4. Fold the paper in half from corner to corner, forming a triangle (broken lines in C).

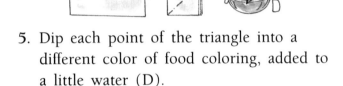

5. Dip each point of the triangle into a different color of food coloring, added to a little water (D).
6. When dry, open the paper.

# ADIRE TIE & DYE
## *West Nigeria*

In West Nigeria in Africa, the ancient craft of dying paper is called adire. Craftspeople dip tied homemade paper into indigo, which is a blue dye that comes from a plant in the pea family.

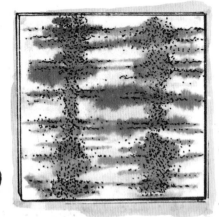

1. Collect your supplies: absorbent papers or paper towels, string, water, blue food coloring, and a bowl.
2. Fold a sheet of paper back and forth using up all the paper (A).
3. Tightly tie string around the folded paper at several places (B).

4. Dip the paper into blue food coloring added to a little water.
5. When dry, remove the strings and open.

# SLITS

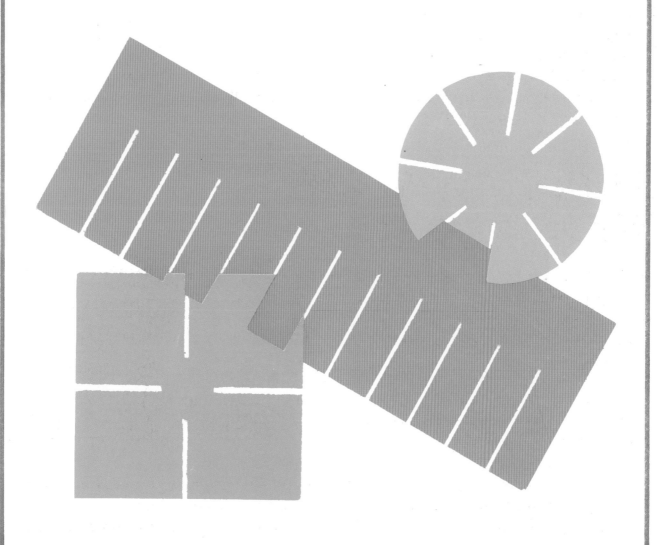

# FLOWER CAGE
## *United States*

No one knows for certain who first created the cobweb cut. In the United States in the mid-1800s, round pullout cobwebs added to valentine cards were called flower cages because pictures of flowers were often hidden underneath.

1. Collect your supplies: paper, printed picture, compass, scissors, string, paper clip, and paste or glue.
2. Using a compass, draw a circle on colored paper. Draw the same size of circle on a picture from a magazine, greeting card, or gift wrap. Cut it out.
3. Cut a paper square larger than the circles.
4. Paste the picture on the square.
5. Fold the other circle in half (A) and in half two more times (B and C).
6. On a folded side near the curved end, make a curved cut. It should end a little away from the opposite side (D).
7. Make the second cut on the opposite side, a little away from the first (E).
8. Make cuts up to the point (F). Each new cut starts on a different side.
9. Cut away a tiny tip of the paper (arrow in F). Open the paper.
10. Tie a paper clip to string. Feed the string through the middle hole (G and H).
11. Add paste or glue to the edge of the picture (I). Lay the circle on the glue. The paper clip is inside.
12. Pull the string to see the picture.

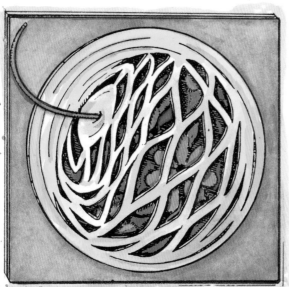

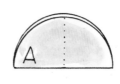

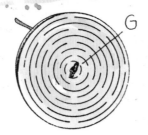

# COBWEB GARLAND
## *China*

For many festivals in China, people decorate the streets with long, colorful cobweb garlands.

1. Collect your supplies: construction or crepe paper, scissors, string, and glue.
2. Fold a large sheet of paper in half and in half again along the length (A).
3. Cut slits into the paper described in the Flower Cage (A). Open the paper.
4. Pull the paper to create a cobweb.
5. Feed string through many cobwebs and hang.

### Three-Dimensional Garland

1. Make many circles described in the Flower Cage.
2. Add four dots of glue on the edge of a circle (B). Place a second circle on it.
3. Add glue to the middle of the second circle (C). Place a circle on it.
4. Continue gluing on circles as you did the first two. Hang with string.

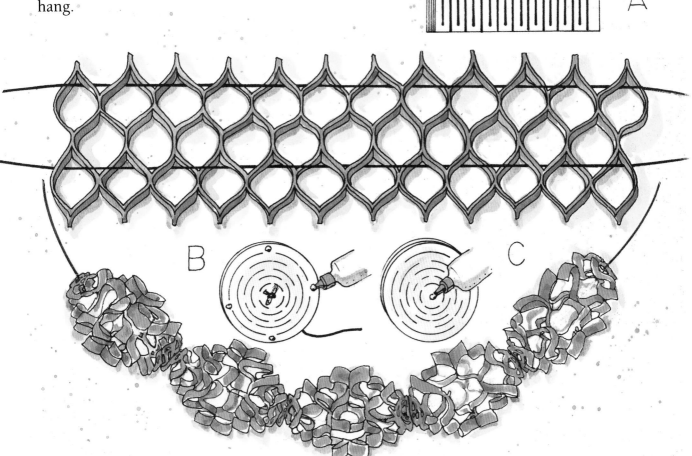

# LANTERN
## *China*

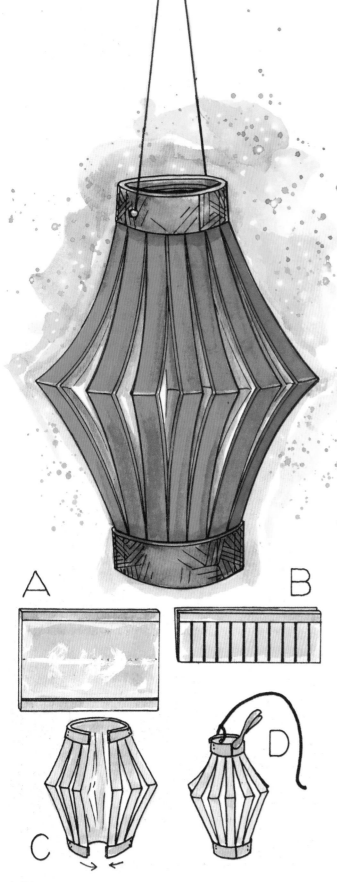

Yuan Hsiao is the festival of lanterns celebrated in China. Lantern shops offer thousands of varieties of lanterns for inside the house and for the garden. With a change in color, the Chinese lantern turns into a lantern with an American touch, the Halloween jack-o'-lantern.

1. Collect your supplies: colored paper, scissors, paste or glue, paper punch, and string.
2. Cut two dark-colored paper strips as long as a sheet of red paper.
3. Glue the strips to the top and bottom of the red paper (A).
4. Fold the paper in half along the length. Make a sharp crease (B).
5. Cut slits into the folded edge up to the strips (B). Open the paper.
6. Roll the paper (C). Paste closed at the top and bottom to form the lantern.
7. Punch two holes into the top of the lantern with a paper punch (D).
8. Tie string into the holes and hang.
9. To make a jack-o'-lantern, roll orange paper in half but do not crease it. Cut slits and paste together as above. Paste on a paper face.

# MAY BASKETS
## *United States*

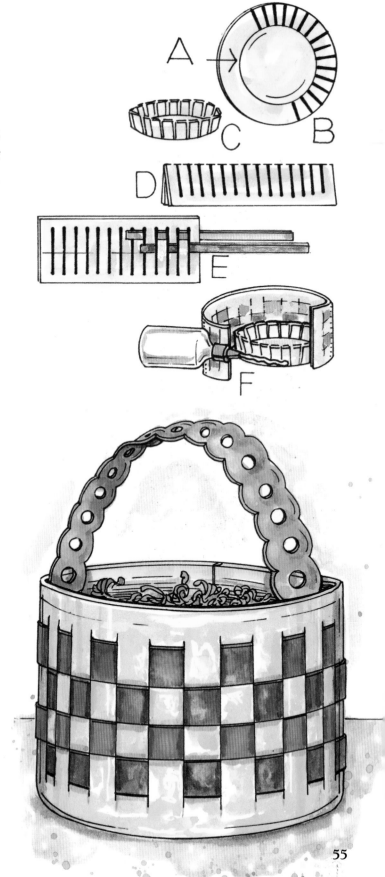

The custom of hanging a gift May basket on a friend's front door at dusk became popular in the United States in the 1800s. Children wove paper baskets and decorated them with paper doilies and ribbons. Then they filled each basket with a piece of candy, a small bunch of flowers, a poem, and the name of the receiver.

1. Collect your supplies: paper, compass, scissors, and paste or glue.
2. Draw a large circle on paper. Cut it out.
3. Draw a circle inside the circle (A).
4. Cut slits close to each other up to the inside circle (B).
5. Fold up the slitted paper to form tabs (C). This is the bottom of the basket.
6. Cut paper long enough to wrap around the bottom, plus a little extra. You may have to glue two sheets together.
7. Fold the paper in half along the length.
8. Cut slits into the folded side (study D). Open the paper.
9. Weave narrow paper strips (or ribbons) through the slits as you would for a basket (study E). Each new strip reverses the in-and-out pattern.
10. Add glue to the tabs of the bottom of the basket (F).
11. Roll the woven paper onto the glued tabs. Glue the sides closed.
12. Glue a fancy paper handle to the inside of the basket. Add Easter grass.

# FRILLS
## *France*

Food preparation in French restaurants is an art. Frills, sometimes called ruffs, decorate poultry legs, pork chops, and ribs.

1. Collect your supplies: white paper, scissors, and paste.
2. Cut a long piece of paper. Make the width twice the size of your middle finger.
3. Fold the paper in half along the length.

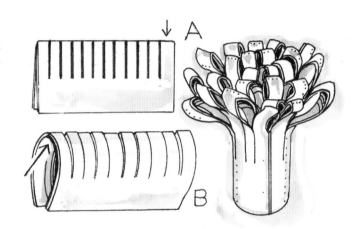

4. Cut slits on the folded side, halfway into the paper (A). Open the paper.
5. With the outside fold (arrow in A) on the inside (arrow in B), roll the paper around your finger. Paste closed.

# POMPONS
## *United States*

Cheerleaders shaking pompons at sporting events is as American as apple pie.

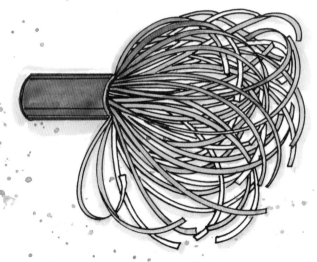

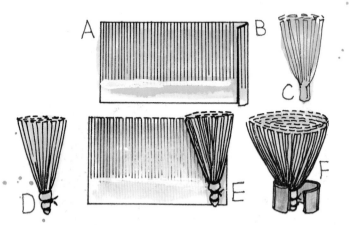

1. Collect your supplies: crepe paper, scissors, string, construction paper, and paste.
2. Cut crepe paper into sheets the same size.
3. Cut slits very close to each other into a sheet to form a fringe (A). Leave some paper uncut for the handle.
4. Roll the paper around itself (B) using up all the paper (C).
5. Tie the handle together with string (D).
6. Wrap another fringed sheet around the tied paper (E). Tie.
7. Add more sheets to make the pompon full.
8. Paste a paper strip over the handle (F).

# INTERLOCKING BELLS
## *Germany*

The tradition of the Christmas tree began in Germany. The first tree ornaments were apples and nuts painted gold, raisins tied in paper, and small toys. Small wax candles provided light. Through the years, the German people added glass and paper ornaments to the tree. Interlocking bells are traditional paper ornaments.

1. Collect your supplies: colored paper, pencil, scissors, and string.
2. Draw two identical bells on paper. Cut them out.
3. Cut a slit a little more than halfway into each bell. On one bell the slit is at the top (A), and on the other bell it is at the bottom (B).
4. Make two holes into the top of a bell using the pencil point.
5. Join the bells together by pushing one slit into the other (C).
6. Tie string into the holes and hang. Make other holiday decorations like a Christmas tree, a Valentine's Day heart, a St. Patrick's Day shamrock, and a Halloween pumpkin.

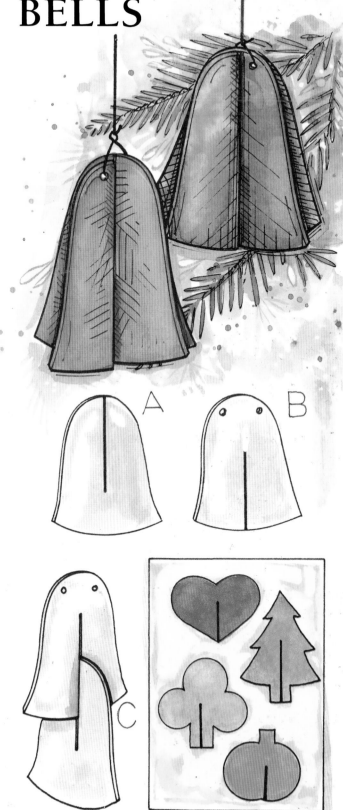

# WOVEN HEART
## *Denmark*

Paper and straw ornaments are traditional Christmas tree decorations in Denmark. Children enjoy making the red and white woven heart that opens up into a small basket. At first, the weaving might be tricky, so ask an adult for help. But once you learn how to weave, you will be able to create not only tree decorations, but special valentines.

1. Collect your supplies: colored paper, pencil, and scissors.
2. Cut two strips of paper the same size, one red and one white. They should be four times longer than they are wide.
3. Fold each paper in half across the width.
4. Draw a curved line at the unfolded end of each paper (A). Cut out the shape.
5. Cut two slits equally spaced into the folded side of each paper. Cut almost up to the curved edge (B).
6. With light pencil lines, mark strips 1, 2, and 3 on the white paper (B).
7. Place the red and the white heart at an angle with each other (study C).
8. Weave the first red strip (marked X) with the white strips: 1 goes through X, X goes through 2, and 3 goes through X (study C).
9. Weave the second red strip (marked Y) with the white strips: Y goes through 1, 2 goes through Y, and Y goes through 3 (study D).
10. Weave the third red strip (marked Z) with the white strips. Repeat as you did the first strip. (Study E.)
11. Pull the papers to tighten the weave.

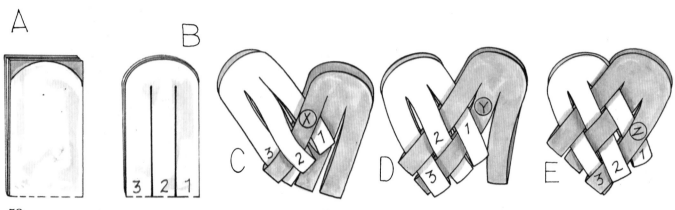

# STRIPS

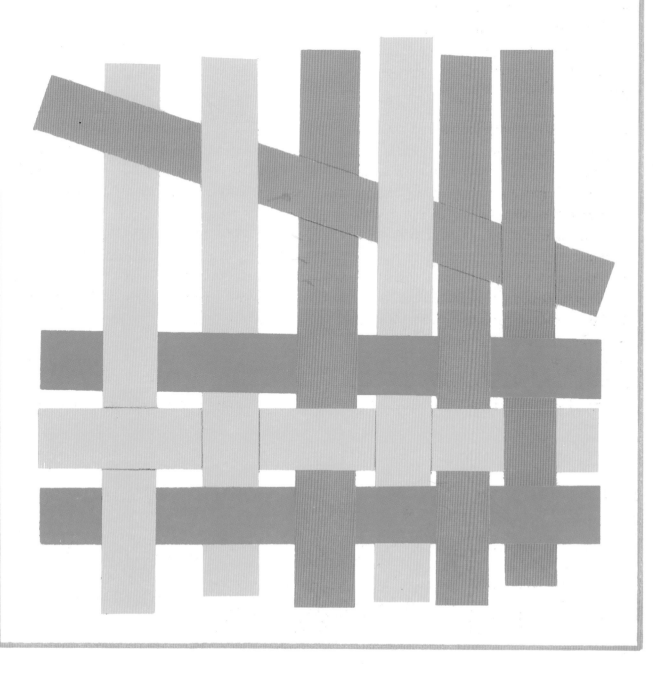

# ST. BRIDGET'S CROSS
## *Ireland*

According to Irish legend, a lass named Bridget was very kind. She made unusual woven crosses tied with ribbons. She gave them as gifts, along with words of love, to whomever she met.

1. Collect your supplies: colored paper, scissors, paste, and ribbon.
2. Cut eight very narrow and very long strips of paper.
3. Loop the strips and paste the ends together.
4. Slip the ends of strip 1 through the loop of strip 2. Slip the loop of strip 3 through loop of strip 1. (Study A.)
5. Slip the ends of strip 4 through the loop of strip 3. Slip the ends of strip 2 through the loop of strip 4. (Study B.)
6. Pull the strips to form a weave in the middle. (Study C.)
7. If you wish to make a double weave cross, follow the weaving directions in D, E, F, G, and H.
8. Tie the ends of the single or double weave cross with ribbon.

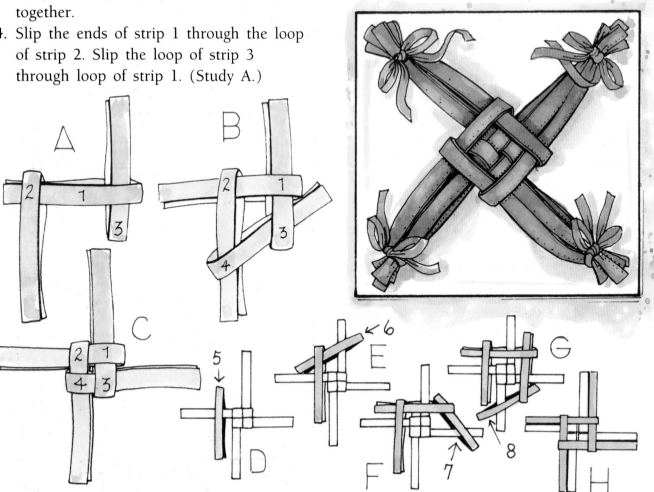

# HEART-IN-HAND
## *United States*

The earliest American valentines were handmade woven paper hearts. It was the custom in the early 1800s to send a sweetheart a valentine, like the heart-in-hand, without revealing the name of the sender.

1. Collect your supplies: colored paper, pencil, scissors, and paste.
2. Trace your hand on paper. Cut it out.
3. Cut red paper into a square to fit on the hand. Fold the square in half.
4. Draw half a heart on the fold (A). Draw several lines and a triangle (study A).
5. Cut out the heart. Cut along the lines to form slits. Cut out the triangle. Open the heart (B).
6. Cut very narrow white paper strips.
7. Weave the strips in and out of the slits on the heart (C).
8. Fold over the bottom edge of the hand (arrow in D). Cut short slits into the fold (D). Unfold.
9. Weave a paper strip with rounded ends through slits on the hand (E).
10. With the good side of the weave facing up, paste the heart to the hand (F).

# CATERPILLAR
## *The Orient*

For as long as there has been paper, children have woven two paper strips in a simple back-and-forth weaving to form slithery snakes and crawly caterpillars. This weaving is called the caterpillar fold. No one knows for certain what country first used the caterpillar fold, although most agree it came from the Orient.

1. Collect your supplies: colored paper, scissors, paste, and crayons or markers.
2. Cut many long strips of paper. They should all be the same width.
3. Paste the ends of two strips together at right angles (study A).
4. Fold strip 1 over strip 2 (B).
5. Fold strip 2 over strip 1 (C).
6. Repeat with strip 1 over strip 2 (D).
7. As you run out of paper, paste new strips to the ends of the first strips (E). Keep adding strips to make a long caterpillar.
8. Paste the ends of the last strips together to finish the caterpillar.
9. Draw a head and tail on paper with crayons or markers. Cut it out.
10. Paste the head and tail to the end of the caterpillar.

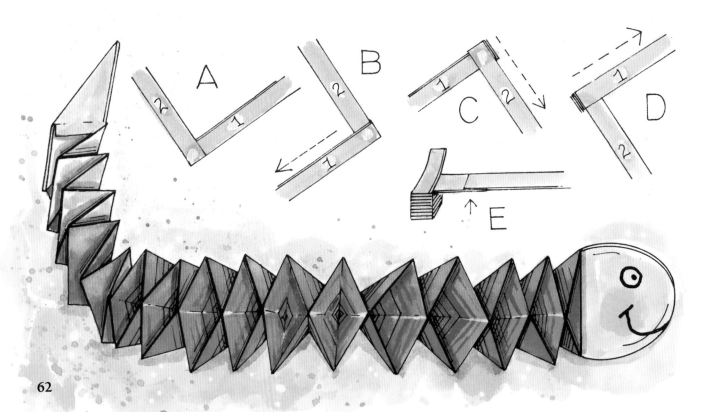

# TANABATA MATSURI CHAINS
## *Japan*

*Tanabata* means "weaving loom." Tanabata Matsuri is a July festival that celebrates the legend of Princess Shokujo and the shepherd boy Kenju, who became stars in the sky. During the festival, long streamers and paper chains that represent the stars in the Milky Way hang in the streets.

1. Collect your supplies: colored paper, scissors, paste, sturdy paper or plastic plate, tape, and string.
2. Cut colored paper into strips of the same size.
3. Roll a strip into a ring and paste it closed.
4. Slip a strip into the ring (A). Paste it closed.
5. Make many long chains of paper rings.
6. Make two holes into a plate.
7. Feed string through the holes and tie the ends together (B).
8. Tape the chains to the inside of the plate (C).
9. Tape a paper decoration on the top of the plate. Hang.

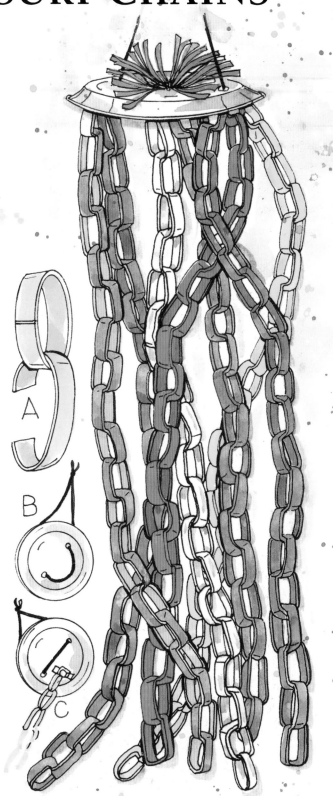

63

# MIZUHIKI
## *Japan*

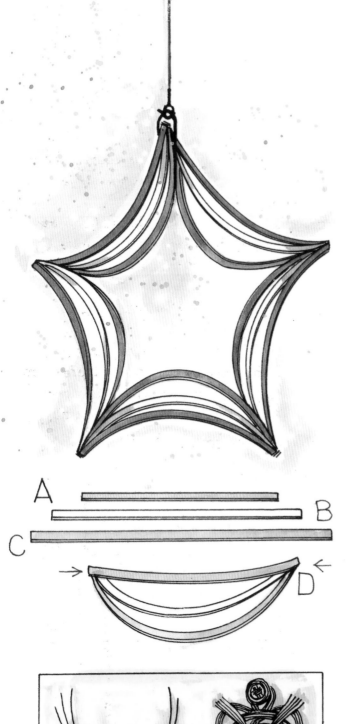

*Mizuhiki,* or "paper strings," are ceremonial decorations made of paper strips as narrow as wrapping cord. Some mizuhiki are fanciful designs, while others are insects, animals, and birds. Gold and silver metallic papers are most popular.

1. Collect your supplies: colored paper, scissors, paste, and string.
2. Cut paper into five, very narrow strips the same length (A).
3. Cut five more strips a little longer than the first strips (B).
4. Cut five more strips a little longer than the second strips (C).
5. Paste the ends of a short, medium, and long strip together to form attached loops (D). Do the same with the remaining strips, making five attached loops in all.
6. Paste the loops together to form a star. The deepest loops are inside the star.
7. Tie string to the star and hang.

# HONEYCOMB
## *China*

The honeycomb is a very simple paper craft that looks very complicated. In China, the honeycomb can open into a fan or be the body of a fanciful dragon. During festivals, honeycombs decorate the streets and blow in the wind.

1. Collect your supplies: colored tissue or lightweight paper, scissors, and paste or glue.
2. Cut many long paper rectangles, all the same size.
3. Add lines of glue or paste near the short sides of one rectangle (arrows in A). Add more lines of glue or paste between the first two. They should be equally spaced.
4. Place a second rectangle on the glued rectangle (B).
5. Add new lines of glue or paste. These are centered between the first lines of glue, which you can clearly see on the paper (C).
6. Place a third rectangle on the glued paper rectangle (D).
7. Repeat the first set of glue lines (E), then the second, and so on, adding new rectangles as you go. The more sheets you add, the higher the honeycomb.
8. Open the paper when dry.

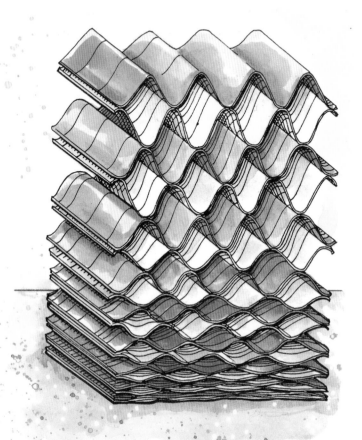

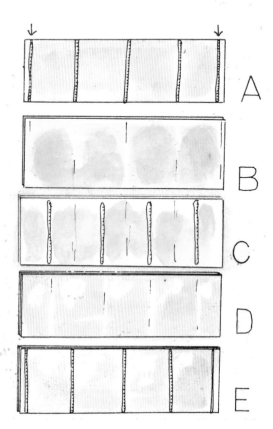

# PEASANT STAFFS
## *Hungary & Romania*

In Hungary weddings are important celebrations. The bridegroom does a traditional dance while twirling a decorated stick that represents a shepherd's staff. The flowers on the staff are a sign of strength. The paper ribbons are in the national colors of red, white, and green.

In Romania, girls contribute gifts to Turca the goat, carried by groups of men in traditional costumes on New Year's Day. The leader of the group carries a tall shepherd's staff, decorated with paper flowers and ribbons.

1. Collect your supplies: crepe paper, scissors, thin wire, wooden dowel, and crepe-paper streamers.
2. For each flower, gather three different sizes of circles in the middle and tie them together with a length of wire (A and B).
3. Wire several flowers to the top of a wooden dowel. You can also use a twig.
4. Tie crepe-paper streamers to the top of the dowel.

**Party Table Centerpiece**
Stand the staff in a coffee can filled with salt and wrapped in colored paper.

**Maypole**
Stand two broom handles taped together in a large can filled with plaster of Paris. When the plaster has set, add long crepe-paper streamers.

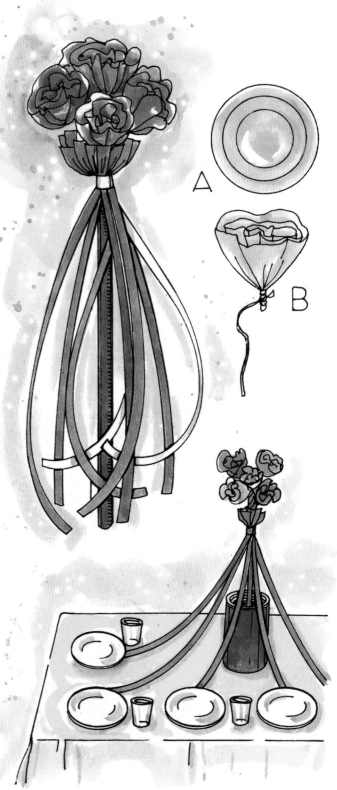

# ROLL-UPS

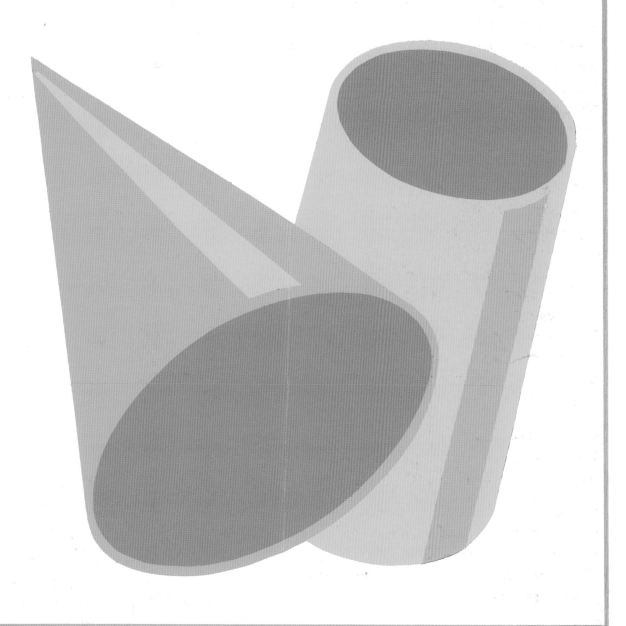

# PAPER BEADS
## *England*

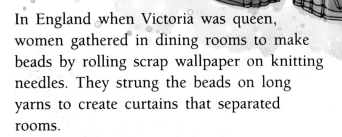

In England when Victoria was queen, women gathered in dining rooms to make beads by rolling scrap wallpaper on knitting needles. They strung the beads on long yarns to create curtains that separated rooms.

1. Gather your supplies: magazine pictures, colored paper, pencil, ruler, scissors, drinking straws, paste, and thread.
2. From colored paper or magazine pictures, cut long triangles about the size of the triangle shown. You can trace the triangle from the book for a pattern.
3. Cover one side of a triangle with paste. Do not paste the picture side of triangles cut from magazines.
4. Place the triangle's glued short side on a drinking straw (A).
5. Wrap the paper completely around itself on the straw (B).
6. Cut away the straw at both ends of the rolled paper (see broken lines in B).
7. For different shapes of beads, cut paper like the examples shown.
8. String the beads on strong thread. Knot the ends of the thread together.

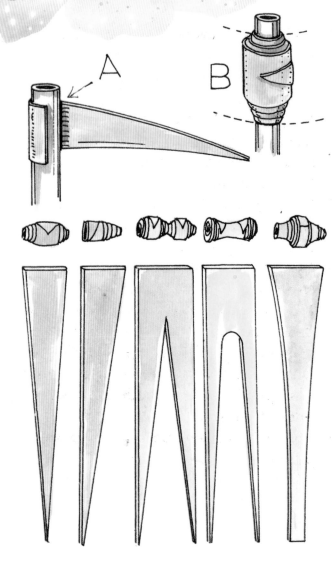

# QUILLING
## *Italy*

Quilling was first done in the 1600s by Italian nuns. It was first called *quillwork* because the nuns rolled strips of paper into curlicue shapes around a large feather called a quill. This craft moved to France, then England where women gathered to create fancy works of art. Quilling came to America before the American Revolution.

1. Collect your supplies: colored paper, scissors, toothpick, and glue.
2. Cut very narrow strips from different colored papers.
3. Wrap an entire strip tightly around a toothpick. You can also roll the strip around a watercolor brush.
4. Remove the toothpick.
5. Paste the end of the strip to the curled circle (A). For a larger circle, loosen the curl before pasting.
6. Create different shapes starting with a circle. Raindrop (B)—pinch once. Heart (C)—pinch one side, push in, and pinch the opposite side. Leaf (D)—pinch opposite sides. V shapes (E and F)—roll the ends of folded strips facing in or out. S shape (G)—roll the ends on opposite sides of the strip.
7. Glue quilled shapes on paper to create a picture.

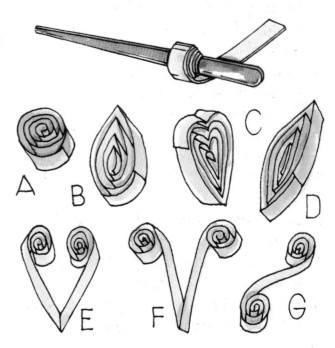

# HOOPSKIRT DOLL
## *Mexico*

Children in many countries enjoy playing with paper dolls. Most paper dolls are flat with attachable clothing. Mexican paper dolls are different because they stand on rolled hoopskirts. Although paper dolls in regional costumes are sold in packages, Mexican children enjoy making their own.

1. Collect your supplies: colored paper, compass, ruler, pencil, scissors, paste, and crayons or markers.
2. Draw a large circle on paper with a compass. You can trace around a plate
3. With a ruler, draw a line across the middle of the circle. Cut the circle in half to form two skirts.
4. Draw a head with a long neck on paper. Cut out.
5. Paste the head on the middle of the straight side of the skirt.
6. Turn the paper over. Draw a face on the head and designs on the skirt with crayon or markers (A).
7. Draw a very long curved shawl on paper (study B). Cut out.
8. Roll the skirt into a cone (C). Paste in place.
9. Roll the shawl and paste the points together (D).
10. Slip the shawl over the doll's head.

# CURLICUE BIRDS
## *Mexico*

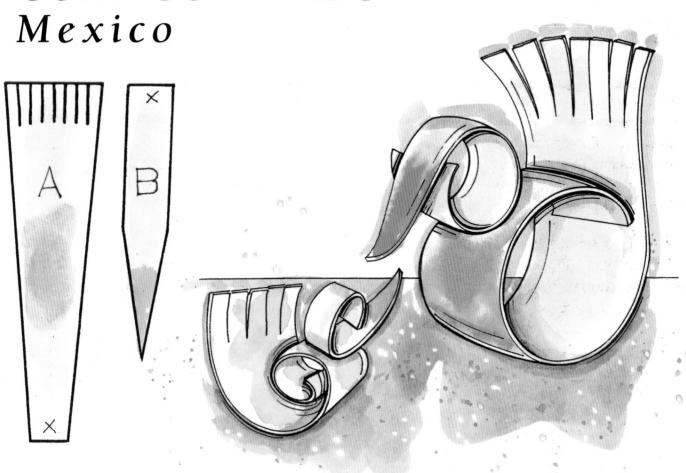

Sometimes the simplest rolled paper can turn into amazing paper sculptures. These rolled birds, used as decorations during party celebrations, come from Mexico.

1. Collect your supplies: paper, pencil, ruler, scissors, watercolor paints, paintbrush, glass of water, and paste.
2. Draw shapes A and B on paper. When rolled, shape A is the body and shape B is the head. For bigger birds, draw larger shapes. Cut out.
3. Cut slits into the wide end of shape A.
4. Paint the papers with watercolor paints.
5. Roll the ends of shape A and shape B marked *x* tightly around a pencil, to curl the papers.
6. To make the body, paste the curled end of shape A just below the tail.
7. To make the head, paste the curled end of shape B just below the beak.
8. Paste the head to the body.
9. To create different birds, cut fancy tails, make longer or wider heads and body shapes, loosen or tighten the curls, and turn the heads in different directions.

# FIRST-DAY SCHOOL CONES
## *Germany*

Entering the first grade in Germany is a special day for German children. On that day, parents give their children a giant cone filled with cookies, candies, and small toys. The cones, sold in stores or made by parents, have colorful decorations. Some cones are as tall as the first graders receiving them. A first-day school cone is a fun birthday gift to make.

1. Collect your supplies: colored poster board, tape, glue, lace, colored paper or markers, package of crepe paper, goodies, and ribbon.
2. Roll a sheet of poster board into a narrow cone. Tape in place (A).
3. Cut the top of the cone to make a round opening (broken lines in A).
4. Glue lace around the top of the cone (B). You can also use cut-up paper doilies.
5. Decorate the cone with drawn or glued-on paper designs (C).
6. Fit a piece of crepe paper into the cone with some paper sticking out (D).
7. Glue the paper to the inside of the cone with a few drops of glue.
8. Fill the cone with goodies and tie the paper closed with ribbons (E).

72

# CORNUCOPIAS
## *Germany*

The Christmas tree was first a German tradition. People decorated the earliest trees with egg cups and paper cornucopias filled with sweet lozenges and barley sugar. The trees were called sugar trees.

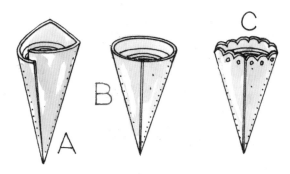

1. Collect your supplies: colored paper, scissors, paste, paper punch, and string.

2. Make small cones described in the First-Day School Cone (A and B). Cut fancy top rims with punched holes (C).
3. Tie on string and fill with candy.

# SANTA LUCIA HAT
## *Sweden*

In Sweden, the Christmas season begins on December 13 with Santa Lucia Day. The oldest girl in the house dresses in white and wears a crown of lingonberry leaves and five lighted candles. Her brother, who accompanies her when she hands out lussekatter buns, wears a tall cone hat and carries a wand.

1. Collect your supplies: colored paper, paste, scissors, tape, and a drinking straw.

2. The hat, with pasted-on stars, is a paper cone that fits on your head.
3. The wand is a star taped to a straw.

# KOKESHI DOLLS
## *Japan*

So important are dolls that they have a special holiday called *Hini Matsuri,* or the "festival of the dolls." Once a year, mothers and daughters remove their beautiful dolls from boxes and display them. Some of these dolls are very elaborate. The *kokeshi* is a simple Japanese doll that has a cylinder body and no arms.

1. Collect your supplies: colored paper, scissors, crayons or markers, and paste.

2. Cut long paper rectangles in different sizes for the bodies.
3. Draw designs on the middle of the papers (A).
4. Roll the papers into cylinders and paste closed (B).
5. Draw heads on paper to fit the bodies (C). Cut out.
6. Paste the heads to the bodies (D).

74

# STICKS

# WIND SPINNERS
## *Ecuador*

The traditional pinwheel is made from a square piece of paper and has four points that catch the breeze. The wind spinner from Ecuador is a pinwheel made from a circle. It has many blades.

1. Collect your supplies: colored paper, compass, scissors, paper punch, metal paper fastener, and plastic drinking straws.
2. With a compass, draw a large circle on paper. Cut out.
3. Drawn a small circle inside the cut-out circle (A). Make a hole in the middle with the point of the compass.
4. Color the inside circle with crayons or markers (B).
5. Cut slits into the paper up to the inside circle (B). At the end of each slit, make a tiny cut along the small drawn circle (see enlargement C).
6. Slightly curl the individual sections on the circle to form blades (D).
7. Flatten the end of a straw and punch a hole into it with a paper punch (E).
8. Push the pinched end of a second straw into the straw with the hole (F).
9. Push the ends of a paper fastener through the hole in the middle of the spinner (G). The blades face out.
10. Push the ends of the fastener through the hole in the straw and open (H).

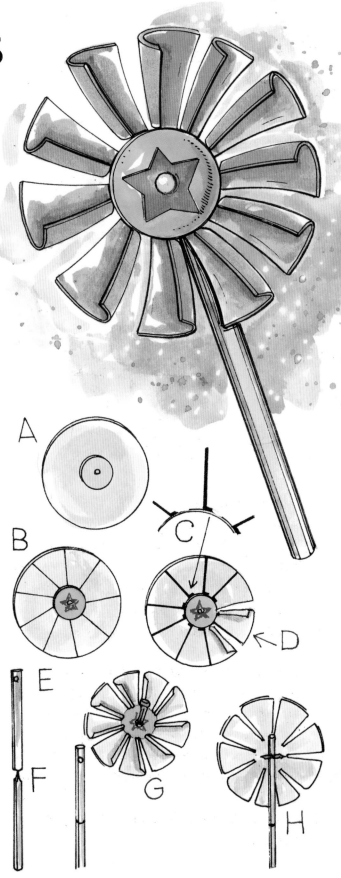

# BANGER
## *China*

Children around the world love to use noisemakers during celebrations, like hitting pots on New Year's Eve and blowing horns at birthday parties. During the Chinese New Year, making noise is a must. Children add the beating sounds of bangers to the popping of exploding firecrackers.

1. Collect your supplies: colored paper, corrugated cardboard, compass, paste, crayons or markers, pencil, string, and two large beads or metal washers.
2. Draw three circles the same size, two on paper and one on corrugated cardboard. Cut out.
3. Draw a different face on each paper circle (A).
4. Paste a face on each side of the cardboard circle (B).
5. Make a hole on each side of the face by carefully twisting the sharpened point of a pencil through all layers (C).
6. Cut two pieces of yarn. The yarn should be as long as the width (diameter) of the circle.
7. Tie an end of each yarn to a hole at the edge of the face. Tie a bead or washer to the other end of each yarn.
8. Push a pencil into the edge of the corrugated cardboard below the face. Glue.
9. Hold the pencil and twist your wrist to make the beads hit the faces in front and back.

# KOI-NOBORI CARP
## *Japan*

On the day of the Iris Festival in Japan, families celebrate the Boy's Festival called Koi-Nobori. Each boy displays a large cloth or paper fish, a carp, on a bamboo pole outside his home. The number of carp tells how many boys are in the family. The carp symbolizes courage and endurance.

1. Collect your supplies: large sheets of paper, pencil, poster paints, cup of water, paintbrush, scissors, paste or glue, string, wooden dowel or pole.
2. Draw a fish on a large sheet of paper with crayons or markers (A). Cut out.
3. Use the fish as a pattern to make a second fish facing the other direction.
4. Glue or paste the two fish together along the top and bottom edges (B). Do not glue the end of the mouth and tail.
5. Make a small hole on each side of the mouth.
6. Tie string into the holes. Tie the fish to a dowel or pole.

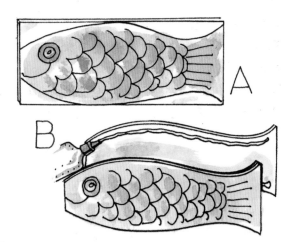

78

# VENETIAN MASK
## *Italy*

Venice is an Italian city built on a group of islands. The houses are very colorful and the streets are water. In the 1700s, Venetians often held masked balls. People dressed in beautiful clothes or costumes and wore fanciful masks. Because the hair styles and hats were big, they attached their masks to sticks, instead of wearing them around their heads.

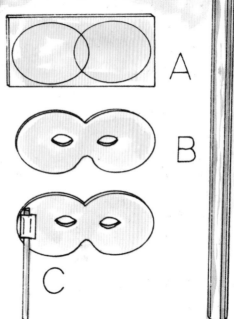

1. Collect your supplies: colored paper, pencil, scissors, plastic drinking straw, tape, feathers, sequins, glitter, and glue.
2. Cut a paper rectangle to the size of your mask.
3. Draw two overlapping ovals on the rectangle (study A).
4. Cut out the connected ovals.
5. Cut out eye openings where your eyes will fall on the mask (B).
6. Tape a straw to one side of the mask (C).
7. Glue on paper cutouts, sequins, glitter, and feathers.

# ADVERTISEMENT FAN
## *United States*

Advertising a product is as American as baseball. A giveaway fan that advertised local stores, businesses, and politicians became popular in the early 1900s. A pretty picture was on one side and the advertisement on the other. Before the invention of the electric fan and air-conditioning, people loved fans during hot summers.

1. Collect your supplies: poster board, pencil, scissors, crayons or markers, ice-cream sticks, and glue.

2. Draw a fan on poster board similar to one of the fans shown. Fan A includes the handle. Fan B will have an added handle. Cut out.

3. Draw a design on one side of the fan with crayons or markers, or paste on a printed picture from a magazine. Write a message on the other side.

4. For fan A, glue an ice-cream stick to the handle, on the side without the picture. For fan B, glue two ice-cream sticks together with the bottom of the fan between them.

# PEACOCK PLUME
## *Sri Lanka*

The peacock comes from Sri Lanka and India. The bird's plumes are so beautiful that they are in great demand around the world. In Sri Lanka, an island off the coast of India once called Ceylon, peacock feathers are used as decorations during their festivals. Because the decorations outnumber the birds, paper feathers are substitutes for the real plumes.

1. Collect your supplies: plastic drinking straws, colored paper, scissors, and glue.
2. Pinch the end of a straw and push it into the end of another straw (A).
3. Cut two long and narrow blue paper rectangles.
4. On one rectangle, squeeze two lines of glue down the center (B). They should be little more than halfway up and close to each other.
5. Lay an end of the attached straws between the glue lines.
6. Place the other rectangle on the first. Press the paper onto the glue along the sides of the straw (arrows in C). Dry.
7. Glue green and yellow paper raindrop shapes on the paper where the top of the straw falls (D).
8. Cut the top of the paper in a curve and cut away the bottom corners (gray areas in D).
9. Cut slits completely around the blue paper to form the feather (E).

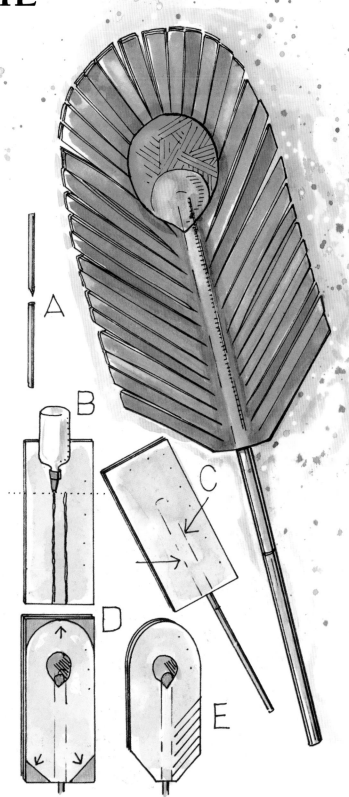

# SHADOW PUPPET
## *Indonesia*

India and China were the first to perform the shadow play, but Indonesia, once called Java, is the most famous for it. The person who works the puppets and tells the story is called the *dalang*. A light behind the puppets, worked behind a screen, casts a colored moving shadow on the screen.

1. Collect your supplies: poster board, pencil, paper punch, scissors, crayons or markers, metal paper fasteners, drinking straws, and tape.
2. Draw the body of a bunny on paper. Include the face and one arm (A).
3. Draw the other arm in two sections (B).
4. Cut out the body and arms.
5. With a paper punch, make a hole in the bunny and holes in the arm sections (study arrows in B).
6. Make two long straw poles. To make a pole, pinch both ends of a straw and push each end into two other straws.
7. Attach the arm sections together with a paper fastener. Attach the arm to the body with another fastener (C).
8. On the back of the bunny, tape one pole to the hand (D) and the other to the feet (E).
9. Paste a paper carrot on the hand.
10. To work the puppet, hold the body pole while you move the arm pole.

# CONSTRUCTIONS

# GOURD DOLL
## *Czech Republic & Slovakia*

Czech and Slovak farmers used to make dolls for their children, with a gourd for the body and strung berries for the arms and legs. A small potato was the head. Today gourd dolls have papier-mâché bodies. Beads take the place of the berries and potato.

1. Collect your supplies: newspaper, paste, gourd, big nail, knife, string, beads, Ping-Pong or foam ball, paper clip, poster paints, and paintbrush.
2. Tear newspaper into tiny strips.
3. Add paste to one side of a strip and lay it on a gourd. Cover the gourd with three layers of pasted strips (A). Dry.
4. Using a big nail, make holes through the paper where the arms and legs will be (A). Ask an adult to help you.
5. Cut through the paper, forming two equal sections, and remove from the gourd (B). Ask an adult to help.
6. For the arms and legs, tie the ends of four strings to paper clips. Feed the other ends of the strings through the holes on each body section (C).
7. Add beads to the strings (D). Tie the ends of the strings to the last beads.
8. For the head, tie a paper clip to a long string. Add a large bead, a small foam ball, or a Ping-Pong ball (E). Ask an adult to help.
9. Close the two body sections over the paper clip (F). Attach them together with glued paper strips.
10. Paint the body with poster paints. Paint a face on the head.

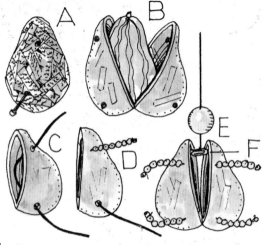

# EASTER ROOSTER
## *Russia*

Decorating eggs for Easter is a craft enjoyed by children in many countries. Russian children turn eggs into strutting roosters, the rulers of the barnyard.

1. Collect your supplies: tracing paper, pencil, scissors, paper, crayons or markers, paste, egg, and food coloring or egg dyes.
2. Fold a sheet of paper in half.
3. Draw the rooster's head and tail (A and B), with the top of each on the fold. You can trace the head and tail from the book for patterns.
4. Cut out the head and tail.
5. Color the head and tail with crayons or markers. Draw feathers and eyes.
6. Dye a hard-boiled egg in red food coloring or Easter dye.
7. Paste the folded head over the wide end of the egg (C). Paste the folded tail over the pointy end (D).
8. Draw the rooster's legs and grass on a long strip of paper.
9. Roll the paper into a ring and paste. The ring should be small enough for the egg to rest on top of it.

# DARUMA DOLL
## *Japan*

There is a legend in Japan that Daruma, an Indian monk in the 1500s, sat thinking in one spot for so many years that his legs withered away. When Daruma was ready to teach others, he had to roll all the way from India to Japan. Japanese children play with a tilting doll that resembles Daruma.

1. Collect your supplies: 4-inch foam ball, knife, spoon, rock, glue, paper, 8-ounce paper cup, and crayons or markers.
2. Cut a small slice off the foam ball (A).
3. On the flat side, scoop out a hole large enough to hold a rock (B).
4. Fit a rock into the hole. Squeeze a lot of glue around it (C). Dry.
5. For a pointy Daruma, roll paper into a cone and glue in place (D). Trim the bottom so the cone fits snugly on the ball. For a flat-top Daruma, cover a paper cup with paper.
6. Draw or glue a face and designs on the cone or cup (E).
7. Add glue to the inside edge of the cone or cup (F).
8. Press the cone or cup on the ball, over the hole (G). The Daruma should stand straight. Dry.
9. When you push the Daruma over, it will return upright.

# NEW YEAR'S DRAGON
## *China*

The Chinese New Year, Yuan Tan, lasts for seven days in late January or in February. The dragon is a symbol of the New Year's celebration. During the holiday, a long paper dragon dances down the streets. Sparkling dragon heads hang in restaurants and public buildings to bring good luck.

1. Collect your supplies: colored paper, pencil, scissors, paste, ribbon, tape, and string.
2. Draw a large heart on paper for the face. Cut out.
3. Paste paper eyes, teeth, and nose on the face (A).
4. Paste a pointy hat and ribbons on the back of the face (study B).
5. Cut five large paper ovals. Cut out a wedge at one end of each (C).
6. On the top back side, paste two ovals with the niched triangles facing up (D).
7. Paste three more ovals on the bottom of the back side, with the niched triangles facedown (E).
8. Glue ribbons to the bottom ovals (E).
9. Decorate the front of the dragon with paper circles.
10. Tape string on the back and hang.

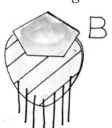

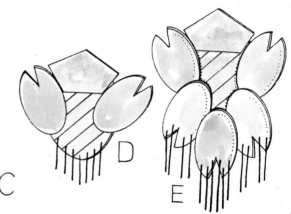

A

B

C

D

E

# DULCE SEÑORITA
## *Guatemala*

*Dulce* is the Spanish word for "sweet." This frilly party centerpiece from Guatemala gets its name from the sweet candy hidden inside.

1. Collect your supplies: colored paper or poster board, tape, scissors, candy, glue, pipe cleaners, and crayons or markers.
2. Roll paper or poster board into a cone and tape in place (A).
3. Trim the open end of the cone so that it stands straight (broken line in A).
4. Cut slits into the cone, around the open end (B). They should be close together.
5. Fill the cone with candy.
6. Fold over the slitted paper to form tabs (C).
7. Glue on the tabs a circle that is a little larger than the open end (D).
8. Add a paper ring to the point for a hat. Tape on pipe-cleaner arms. Glue on paper hands (E).
9. Draw a face on the cone between the arms and the hat with crayons or markers.
10. Cut slits along several colored paper strips (F). Slightly curl the strips.
11. Starting at the bottom, wrap the strips around the cone and tape at the back (G). Add strips to the point.

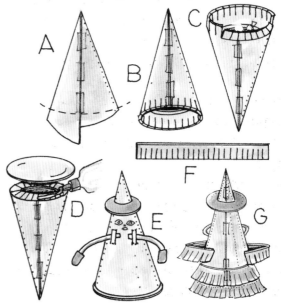

# PIÑATA
## *Mexico*

During the nine days before Christmas, Mexican families hold posada parties. Children carrying clay figures of Mary and Joseph knock on doors and join the parties. During the holiday, children break the piñata, a large pottery jar decorated with crepe paper. The candy, nuts, fruits, and toys fall out when the jar is broken. Piñatas are popular at other times of year, too.

1. Collect your supplies: large grocery bag, wrapped candy, small toys, newspaper, cord, colored paper, tape, and crepe paper.
2. Put candy and toys into the bag. Add crumpled newspaper to fill out the bag.
3. Gather the top of the bag and tie it closed with a long length of cord (A).
4. Roll four sheets of paper into cones and tape them in place (B).
5. Trim the bottom of the cones (C).
6. Cut slits into sheets of crepe paper to form long fringes.
7. Roll the fringes around the points of the cones (D). Tape in place.
8. Tape the cones to the bag (E).
9. Make a fringe for the bottom of the bag and tape in place.
10. To play, hang the piñata from a tree or on a broomstick. Blindfolded players try to break the piñata with a stick.

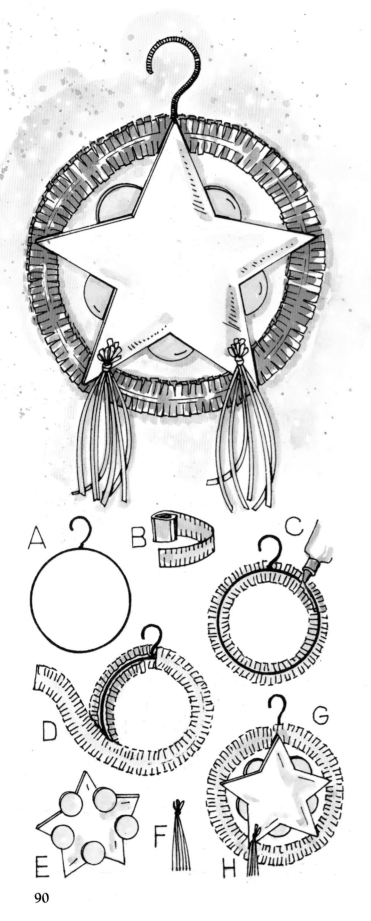

# FAROL STAR
## *Spain*

The farol star first started as a Christmas custom in Spain. Groups of singers called minstrels carried beautiful paper stars when they entertained the Spanish nobility. Spain brought the farol to the Philippines, where it is still part of the Filipino Christmas.

1. Collect your supplies: wire coat hanger, crepe-paper streamer, scissors, glue, colored paper, and ribbon.
2. Ask an adult to shape a wire hanger into a circle (A).
3. Cut slits into both sides of two paper streamers (B). The streamers should be long enough to wrap around the circle.
4. On a table, form a ring with a streamer.
5. Place the hanger on the ring (C).
6. Squeeze glue on both sides of the hanger on the streamer (C).
7. Lay the other streamer on the ring (D). Press it onto the glued hanger.
8. Cut a paper star to fit on the ring. Paste circles between the points (E).
9. Tie ribbons into two tassels (F).
10. Glue the star to the crepe-paper ring with a point at the top. The circles are on the underside (G).
11. Glue the tassels to the star (H).

# STAR MOBILE
## *Denmark*

The Scandinavian countries of Sweden, Norway, and Denmark have Christmas tree ornaments made from paper and straw. The six-pointed star is a popular symbol of the holiday. This mobile, made with red and green paper and plastic straws, is a fun Christmas decoration. Change the papers to blue and white and you have a mobile for Chanukah.

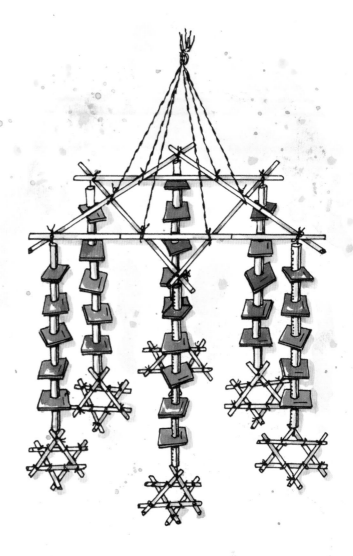

1. Collect your supplies: plastic drinking straws, scissors, paper punch, string, paper, and paste.
2. Cut twelve drinking straws into three equal sections (A).
3. Press flat the ends of each straw. Make a hole in both ends with a paper punch.
4. Tie every three straws into triangles with string through the holes (B).
5. Tie every two triangles together to form six-pointed stars (C).
6. The mobile's frame is a large star made as above. To make a pole, pinch both ends of a straw and push them into two other straws (D). Make six.
7. To make beads, wrap narrow strips of paper around a straw and paste in place (E). Slip the beads off the straw.
8. Tie a long string to each small star. String on beads and paper squares.
9. Tie the strings of beads and stars to the points of the frame.
10. Tie string to the frame and hang.

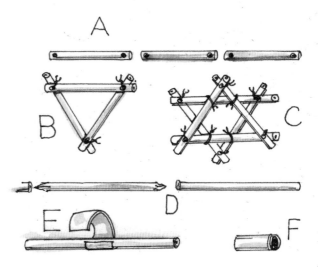

91

# PARTY FAVOR
## *Peru*

In South American countries, parties are often given outdoors, from backyard patios to city parks. Paper decorations dress not only tables, but also trees and bushes. It is a tradition to give guests a party favor to take home. This pot of posies comes from Lima, Peru.

1. Collect your supplies: paper cup, colored paper, glue, scissors, piece of play clay, and pipe cleaners.
2. Wrap paper around a paper cup and glue in place (A).
3. Trim away the extra paper at the top and bottom of the cup (B).
4. Pinch the top of the cup so that it looks more like a square than a circle (C).
5. Cut paper leaves and flowers (D).
6. Cut pipe cleaners in half.
7. Glue the pipe cleaners to the leaves and flowers (E).
8. Twist the pipe cleaners on the flowers and leaves around an uncut pipe cleaner (F).
9. Place a small ball of play clay (or craft foam) into the cup (G). Push the bunch of flowers into the clay.

# FLOWER SPRAY
## *Portugal*

In Portugal, people use flowers for both happy and sad occasions. Floral sprays made of colored and gold metallic paper are popular decorations for doors, especially for weddings. Paper flowers are very fancy with embossing and beadwork. Bows are often made of crepe-paper streamers.

1. Collect your supplies: colored paper, scissors, poster board, glue, crepe-paper streamer, and beads.
2. For each flower, cut three sizes of paper circles in different colors.
3. Cut slits into the edge of all the circles (A). Curl the slitted paper.
4. For each flower, paste three circles together with the smallest on top.
5. Cut a pointy design into the edge of two large circles (B).
6. Cut a large oval from poster board (C).
7. Glue cut-out leaves on the oval extending out from the edge (D). Do not add leaves where the bow will be placed.
8. Glue the paper flowers on the oval. Glue a pointy circle in the middle (E).
9. Glue on a crepe-paper streamer bow. Glue the other pointy circle on the knot.
10. If you wish, glue beads on the pointy circles and on the bow.

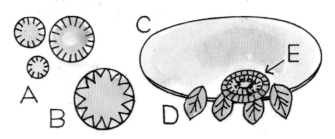

# KLAUSE HEADDRESS
## *Switzerland*

On January 12 in some Swiss villages, people called Klause wear costumes and parade though the streets. The Klause wear bells of all sizes, which jingle as they stomp and dance. Masks cover their faces. They wear on their heads large, silly headdresses. People give coins and presents to the Klause when they dance past their doors.

1. Collect your supplies: cereal box, scissors, colored paper, pencil, glue, tape, milk carton, and a toilet paper tube.
2. Tape the open end of an empty cereal box closed (A).
3. Cut out a hole on the front of the box big enough to fit on your head (B).
4. On colored paper, trace the sides of the box except the one with the hole. The top paper is green.
5. Glue the papers to the box (C).
6. Tape the top end of a milk carton closed. Cut away the bottom (D).
7. Glue paper on the sides of the carton. Add windows, a door, and a folded roof.
8. Cut slits into a long strip of green paper (E). Roll the paper and push it into a cardboard tube to make a tree.
9. Glue the house, tree, basket-grass bushes, and decorations on the top of the box. Glue rectangles on the sides.

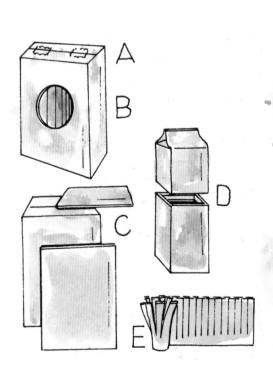

# PAPIER-MÂCHÉ MASKS
## *Multicultural*

The papier-mâché mask has a long history, starting with ancient Greek theater. Through the centuries, people around the world used masks in dances, holidays, and religious celebrations. Here are a clown mask from the American circus, a donkey (burro) mask for Carnaval in El Salvador, and a monk's mask from Tibet.

1. Collect your supplies: round balloon, newspaper, paste, waxed paper, bowl, white glue or wallpaper paste, spoon, sandpaper, poster paints, and string.
2. Blow up a balloon and knot.
3. Tear newspaper into small strips.
4. Lay a strip on waxed paper and cover one side with paste (A).
5. Lay the glued side of the strip on the balloon. Cover the entire balloon with three layers of pasted strips (B).
6. Tear newspaper into tiny pieces. With a spoon, mix the pieces in a bowl with white glue or wallpaper paste (C). If the mixture is too wet, add more newspaper, and if too dry, add more paste.
7. Mold the mixture into eyebrows, nose, mouth, horns, and other facial features.
8. Press the features onto the balloon. Glue in place (D).
9. Dry the balloon mask overnight.
10. Cut the paper on the balloon mask in half (E). Remove the balloon.
11. Make a hole on the sides of the mask (F).
12. Sand the paper smooth with sandpaper and paint with poster paints.

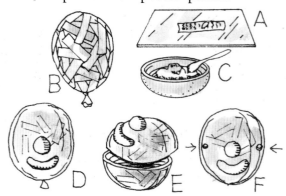

# INDEX